The Natural History of
The Burren

With deepest gratitude from the Burren Spring Conference, 2009
[signature] d'Toole

by
Gordon D'Arcy and
John Hayward

IMMEL
Publishing

The Burren by Gordon D'Arcy and John Hayward

© 1992, 1997 text: Gordon D'Arcy

© 1992 photographs: John Hayward

© Reprinted 2002

Executive Editor: Peter Vine

Editing, design, typesetting: Shirley Kilpatrick, Icon Publications Ltd, Kelso, Scotland
Diagrams and maps: David Woolgrove, Curlew Graphics, Yetholm, Scotland

A CIP catalogue record for this book is available from The British Library

ISBN 1 898162 51 4

IMMEL Publishing Ltd
14 Dover Street,
Mayfair, London WIS, 4LW.
Tel: 207 491 1799
Fax: 207 493 5524

ACKNOWLEDGEMENTS:

I would like to thank the following individuals and organisations for their help and guidance in the preparation of this book. To those whom I have inevitably forgotten I extend my apologies.

First, to John Hayward whose beautiful photographs embellish the book and without whose involvement it would have been an impossibility, I extend my sincere thanks.

To the following individuals who read the text: Donal Murphy, Cilian Roden, Dave McGrath, Noel Kirby.

To Jacinta Reynolds, Miles Carey (Clare County Council) Noel Kirby, Ann Lynch, Tony McCullagh (Office of Public Works), Jim Ryan *et al.* (Wildlife Service, OPW), Noel Lane (Coillte, Department of Forestry), Michael O'Cleary, Martin O'Grady (Department of Fisheries), Nigel Monaghan (National Museum, Geological Section), Paul Gosling (Dept of Archaeology, University College, Galway), Prof. Michael Mitchell (Dept of Botany, UCG), Prof. W. A. Watts (per Daphne Gill, Trinity College, Dublin).

To the libraries of: Trinity College; The Royal Irish Academy; University College Galway; National Library Dublin.

To the National Museum, Dublin: the Ulster Museum, Belfast.

To the following individuals who helped in one way or another: Dymphna Hyland, Brendan and Catherine O'Donoghue, John McNamara, Mr Flemming (Kinvara), Paddy O'Sullivan, Kate McAney, Paddy Sleeman, R. F. Haynes, Michael O'Connell, J. S. Fairley, Brendan Keegan. To my wife Esther Mary I extend my special thanks and last but certainly not least to Lucy for typing the entire text so unstintingly, thanks.

The Natural History of
The Burren

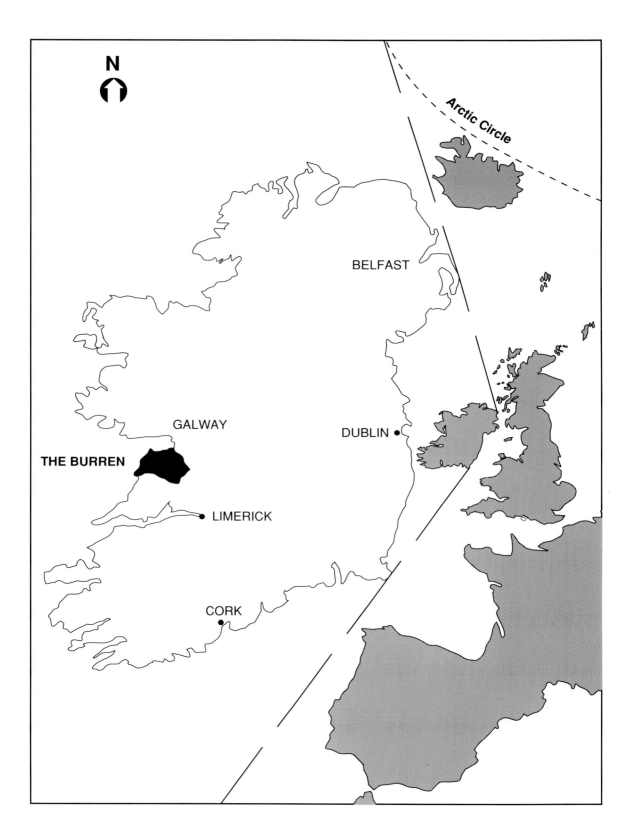

N

Arctic Circle

BELFAST

GALWAY

DUBLIN •

THE BURREN

• LIMERICK

• CORK

Contents

Foreword

Much has already been written about aspects of the Burren's natural history but it lies mainly in academic journals, difficult for the general reader to find. There are, of course, a number of booklets, articles and sections in books relating to the subject but they tend to focus on the wonderful flora and pay little heed to the fauna or the overall natural history.

Though it is hoped that naturalists and other specialists will find this book useful, it is aimed primarily at the interested layperson. It is designed, in its straightforward format and abundant pictorial content to inform the reader of the Burren's natural wonders, their significance and where and at what time to go looking. And the visitor will need to go looking for although some of the flora specialities grow obligingly by the roadside many of the really satisfying discoveries await the rambler.

It would be a pity, however, if a book aimed at publicising this unique environment were to become an instrument in its degradation, either to be used by avaricious collectors to locate and 'scoop' rarities or to feel the effects of the more permanent marks of man on the landscape. An essential element in the book is a plea for conservation both of species and of the region itself. The final chapter on the future of the Burren contains suggestions and recommendations to safeguard and sensitively develop the region's wildlife potential.

This book is a product of the existing literature and my own notes over a five year period. It is not the final word: there is no final word on a dynamic and enigmatic place like the Burren, which unfolds its natural secrets gradually and only to those who notice. I am optimistic that when it comes to revising it, more will have been discovered than has been lost in the interim.

Gordon D'Arcy

Introduction

A Burren Perspective

he Burren looks a most un-Irish place. The image of the emerald isle propagated abroad by tourist representatives and emigrants does not apply to this grey plateau in north Clare. Nor does it produce the beautiful rivers and verdant pastures so often extolled by visitors from other countries whose landscapes have suffered the ravages of rural despoliation. The Burren has, in fact, more in common with some of the lesser-known regions of Yugoslavia or the mesas of Arizona than with other areas of western Europe, let alone Ireland.

It has been variously described as a 'barren stoney place' (cf the Irish **boíreann**), a limestone desert and a moonscape, and to some degree it is all of these. But perhaps 'fertile rock' is most

Magical Mullaghmore

apposite. It is on the one hand flat and ostensibly bare while on the other it is unbelievably productive and rich.

The perspective is so strange that the Burren may inspire a mixture of feelings. A casual visitor, having 'done' the Burren in a single day may depart with a hint of disappointment, but the visitor for whom time is not an adversary may well become entranced, held in the grip of the place. In this state of mind further investigation is obligatory. Such a mortal must look beneath the surface for the secrets which the Burren holds close to its limestone bosom.

Subterranean conduits echo with rilling water, for this is a superficially dry land, its waterways having retreated into the soluble rock with the passage of time. Only in periods of high precipitation does the groundwater gurgle up through the sink-holes to flood the turloughs (from the Irish **tuar lach** meaning 'dried-up place').

Above ground, sounds are a feature too. It is impossible to ignore the clinks and grunts of the limestone chunks as they talk back to the attentive walker. Many people are inclined to wander this country, fascinated by the myriad fossil traces of long-extinct marine creatures or curious about the soilless pavement strewn with rounded boulders and scarred with deep scratches – legacies of the last Ice Age. Others will be drawn by the question of the apparently treeless topography. The roots of this mystery are now so obscure that the only evidence available lies with minuscule pollen grains trapped in peat-filled fens where they were deposited by a western breeze thousands of years ago. This stratigraphic record has revealed, in core samples, the influence on the landscape of Neolithic man as surely as if it were documented in early script. But the rambler need not be discouraged if this evidence has been obscured by accumulated sediment, for scattered around the terrain are tangible fragments of the story of continuous habitation, a story which has been unfolding for at least five millennia. And a habitat it remains, though less significantly for people: more now for a plethora of other living things.

No cultivated phrase or flowery word can adequately describe the resplendent rock garden that is the Burren throughout the summer. The visitor who comes for whatever reason and departs without having experienced this floral display will have missed a treat not to be found elsewhere. The combination of green, bespangled with yellow, red, purple and white, set against a matt grey background has surely been designed to elevate the spirit. The retina is spared the garish assault of large, excessively cloned, floral varieties but is rather assuaged by the natural subtlety of the display. As with gem-stones, rarity adds an extra dimension: arctic-alpine, montane and Mediterranean plants proliferate amid the familiar. Nor is the display restricted to the limestone proper. Throughout the summer months the Burren's freshwater and coastal wetlands are in flower. Here, a fluctuating water-table, desiccation and other factors result in the delicately zoned character of the vegetation which provides a pleasing backdrop to many of the region's specialities.

Petal-bright insects pollinate many of the flowering plants. Hoverflies, bees, day-flying moths and particularly butterflies catch the eye. With only one or two exceptions all the resident Irish butterflies are to be found in the region-testimony not only to the diversity of plant life but also to the unspoiled conditions prevalent there.

An eye distracted by the brightness of butterflies will also notice the rose-pink breast feathers of the bullfinch calling from the scrub, but it may overlook the cryptic plumage of the nightjar, whose churring call has earned it the colourful Irish name **tuirne lín** (flax-spinning wheel). Other open country summer birds include the wheatear and the cuckoo, both of which are particularly common in the Burren. Kestrels can be seen here too, hovering on high, seeking out terrestrial prey like lizards. By the end of the summer many of these birds will be on their way to African winter quarters. In the Burren's wetlands and along the coast birds which are migrating through or to the Burren for the winter are gathering to take advantage of the rich feeding grounds which the region offers.

The Burren's furry denizens are more elusive than the birds though many like the fox, badger and field mouse are widespread and common. The pine marten, the 'cat' of the Burren is so secretive in its habits that the nocturnal rambler will have to be content with an occasional torchlight glimpse. Herds of feral goats inhabit the upper ground and are a consolation to those who crave wild company on their outings. The shaggy coats, beards and remarkable back-curved twisting horns convey an air of sagacity to the old billies, patriarchs of the herds.

The mammal most regularly encountered along the Burren coastline is the common seal. The grey seal also occurs but less commonly and the otter, while it occurs along much of the coastline, is less familiar owing to its nocturnal habits. Porpoises and dolphins are also seen from time to time. Occasionally also, the extraordinary occurs. Killer whales for instance, wooed inshore from their Atlantic home, have been spotted feeding on the abundant fish stocks off the Burren coast.

It is not, however, the individuality of the Burren's wildlife that render it special: it is rather the interdependence of its various strands. To pursue only the obvious or the easily accessible is to deny oneself a perspective on the matrix of which rock, water, flora and fauna are integral parts. And to look at these elements alone is to ignore the role that man has played in providing the circumstance – albeit unwittingly – whereby this paradise exists.

Man now has the capacity to radically alter the Burren – this 1 percent of the total land surface of Ireland – as he has done with the vast majority of the remainder. Already, there are signs of unsightly and probably unnecessary land clearance; the random construction of incongruous-looking houses complete with Spanish arches and balustrades, random dumping and surface pollution from silage pits, and so on. To date, the effect has been largely peripheral but how much violation can the Burren sustain before it ceases to be the wilderness it is still?

Wouldn't it be a tragic irony – 'a bit Irish', in a way – if this part of Ireland, presently the most un-Irish, were to end up as Irish as the rest?

Burren Beginnings

The Story in the Rock

A walk across the Burren flatlands presents the most amazing paradox, for it is also a walk across an ancient seabed. This limestone plateau was, some 320 million years ago, a squelchy mass of limy mud beneath a warm, tropical sea. In the immensity of the interim, geological forces have converted the mud to rock and lifted it evenly above the sea so that it is now a horizontally bedded mass of Carboniferous limestone. Gone are the younger, overlying sediments – stripped off by the bulldozing action of the glaciers. Beneath, at a depth of about 800 metres (2,500 feet), is a horizontal intrusion of granite, a shelf of Caledonian igneous rock, which seals off the Burren limestones from more ancient sediments. Underfoot, therefore, is a wonderfully preserved record of many millions of years from the Lower Carboniferous era – a geological time capsule from a period at the limits of our imaginations.

But these ancient seas were far from barren. Lumps, bumps and irregular patterns in the otherwise even grey rock are the traces of life-forms which once teemed in these waters. On dying they accumulated in the mud to be exposed, aeons later, as fossils in the rocky surface. It is not difficult to find clearly identifiable fossils of corals – testimony to the warm conditions which existed when they were alive. Most abundant are the multi-branched varieties such as *Lithostrotion* or the single-stalked varieties like *Zaphrentis* and *Caninia* which have a distinctive cellular cross-section.

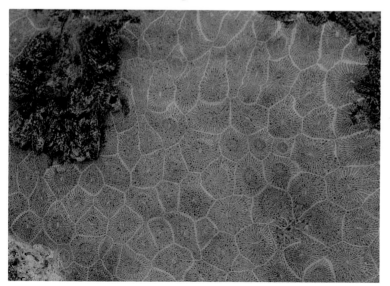

If broken out of the rock, the latter two resemble the discarded horns of some primordial Burren goat. Over parts of the limestone the fossil remains of crinoids (also called sea or stone lilies) can be found. In the rock these fossils look more like cement-covered fragments of a broken necklace than ancient relatives of starfish and sea urchins. Fabric-like patterns in

Cross section through
Lithostrotion coral fossil.

the rock are usually the traces of ancient moss animals (bryozoans) which have similar relatives, sea mats, living in Irish coastal waters today. Bands of black chert are common features in the limestone. These too may have organic origins. Despite the fact that they now reveal no trace of the primitive creatures which formed them, it is thought that these layers are derived from the reconstituted remains of sponges. In the Carboniferous (as today) these creatures fed on plankton which they filtered from the water.

Other kinds of filter-feeders were shelled creatures. Some familiar bivalved molluscs of today, such as cockles (*Cardium*), scallops (*Pecten*) and otter shells (*Lutraria*) had counterparts which can be found as fossils in the Burren's limestones. Some like the lampshells, are less familiar. These brachiopods were not as symmetrical as the cockles, having one of their shells more swollen-looking than the other. An example, now extinct, but found commonly as a fossil in the Burren is the spirifer, which looks rather like a flattened cockle with a central ridge.

Fossil of Carboniferous Gastropod.

Many used the calcium-rich waters to grow coil-shaped shells for protection. These ancient gastropods have modern counterparts in the periwinkles and topshells found commonly on our shores. Like them, they were predominantly creatures which grazed on algae but some, like the whelks, may have been predatory as well. They all coexisted on the seabed amid the jungle of other slow-moving or sedentary organisms and algae.

In the water above, spirally coiled creatures with tentacles, predecessors of octopuses and squids, flitted about in shoals. These were goniatites, early relatives of the ammonites. Were it not for the *Nautilus* which survives today as a representative of these ancient creatures, we would know little now of their free-swimming lifestyle. Goniatite fossils can be found occasionally in the limestone, their coiled form resembling that of the Catherine wheel firework.

The fossils of many of these ancient creatures can be found randomly throughout the Burren, though some places have greater concentrations and variety than others. The many stone walls in the region are good places to look. Here the fossils often stand out as whitish calcite protrusions in the grey rock. They show clearly also in the stonework of older buildings. Fossil-filled blocks appear to have been specially selected in some instances – fitting tablets to the vast timescale represented in the Burren's rock.

The fossil evidence in the limestones of the Burren allows us (at least in our mind's eye) to reconstruct a simple picture of the natural history of the life-filled sea and its muddy bed that was the Burren more than 300 million years ago. It is not, however, within the scope of this book to delve further into these earliest times: it is enough to set the scene and move to more recent times.

Just as a granite intrusion beneath the Burren limestones has obliterated the fossil story from earlier epochs, so the effects of erosion have removed younger, overlying strata, together with their fossil record. The Lower Carboniferous limestones of the Burren are thus a sealed unit – a display cabinet of the natural history of truly ancient times. It is only by correlating the fossil record with that from elsewhere that we can suggest a reconstruction of what might have been had the overlying blanket of shales, flagstones and coal measures remained. These rocks developed from deltaic deposits which ultimately became dry land. It is known that gigantic ferns (*Pecopteris*), horsetails (*Calamites*) and clubmosses (*Lycopsis*) grew on this land: these plants are represented by scaled-down living examples in the Burren today.

An insight into the plant communities which could well have existed on Carboniferous limestone about three million years ago and prior to the Ice Age has been derived from the fossil evidence found in a lignite deposit near Headford, in Galway. The fossil evidence was in the form of pollen and suggests a tree cover representative of a warm climate and somewhat acid conditions. The pollen was from exotic trees like redwoods (*Sequoia*), swamp-cypress (*Taxodium*) and umbrella pine (*Sciadopitys*) and a ground cover of a variety of heathers. This fossil deposit lies in karstic topography about 60 metres above sea level and in circumstances suggestive of the Burren nowadays.

The Ice Age and after

The Ice Age had a profound effect not only on the topography but also on the natural history of the Burren. However, due to the obliterating effect of the successive advances of the glacial ice masses (there were several with discrete warm phases, or interglacials, between), it is only possible now to speculate on the early effects. Most of what is known relates to the final advance of the ice which crossed Galway Bay moving in a generally north-east, south-west direction. It polished smooth the north-facing limestone outcrops like Black Head and Cappanawalla, left deep scratches in the limestone pavement and dumped acres of rounded boulders at its outer edges. It finally melted and retreated about 10,000 years ago.

One of the interglacials has produced an interesting record of the tree cover that existed not

Glacially rounded boulders at Rockforest in the eastern Burren.

far from the Burren about a quarter of a million years ago. This is referred to as the Gortian Warm Stage (from the location in which it was found near Gort). The pollen record from the ancient peaty layer, as revealed by studies of scientists such as Prof. W. A. Watts of Trinity College, Dublin, derived from the vegetation suggests a diverse woodland cover. Initially birch (*Betula*), juniper (*Juniperus*), pine (*Pinus*) and willow (*Salix*) were the significant early invaders. The climax stage was dominated by oak (*Quercus*) and pine with a gradual invasion of holly (*Ilex*), ash (*Fraxinus*), hazel (*Corylus*) and yew (*Taxus*). Fir (*Abies*) and spruce (*Picea*) occurred also – trees not known in Ireland since the end of the Ice Age. Other species known in Ireland now as introductions were recorded then as natives: they include box (*Buxus*) and rhododendron. During such interglacial warm periods (which may have lasted tens of thousands of years at a time) land masses adjoined and extended beyond the boundaries of present-day west and north-west Europe. This enabled not only the spread of plants but also the peregrinations of animals.

Populations of mammals, long established in the Asiatic land mass, migrated westwards and into present-day Ireland. During such migrations weird and wonderful creatures like mammoths (*Mammut*) occurred here. Indeed, a leg bone (humerus) dredged up from Galway Bay in the nineteenth century was thought by some to have been that of a mammoth, though others dismissed it as the leg bone of a circus elephant! Until the advent of a well-defined warm interstadial about 13,000 years ago, there were very long periods in which tundra conditions prevailed. It is now known that a diverse mammalian fauna had become established here by that time. This included arctic mammals like lemmings (*Lemmus*), arctic fox (*Alopex*), reindeer (*Rangifer*) and species from more temperate latitudes like wolf (*Canis lupus*), brown bear (*Ursus arctos*), wild boar (*Sus scrofa*) and wild horse (*Equus*). The giant (Irish) deer (*Megaloceros*), that horse-sized deer with a three metre antler spread, was also a feature of the glacial fauna, though it appears to have died out with the start of the final period of glaciation about 11,000 years ago. A much more familiar animal, the Irish hare, was a probable contemporary of the giant deer which may have managed to survive since that time.

Newhall and Edenvale caves near Ennis (not far to the south of the Burren) have supplied a tantalising glimpse of some of the wildlife that must have been present in the vicinity of north Clare in glacial times. The list includes the species mentioned above, but also the wild cat (*Felis sylvestris*) and the wood (field) mouse (*Apodemus sylvaticus*) whose claim to ancient Irish ancestry is the source of some dispute. In the latter case, particularly, it was thought that the mouse remains found in the material on the cave floor might have been of recent origin, and might, due to the action of flowing water or some other disturbance have become intermixed with the much older glacial remains.

Hibernation pits and bones in the stalagmite floor layer in the Ailwee Cave point to the brown bear having survived in the Burren into post-glacial times. The fauna which inhabits the region today became established following land-bridge invasions from the east, in the first two millennia of the post-glacial period. They comprised carnivores like the stoat (*Mustela erminea*), the badger (*Meles meles*), the fox (*Vulpes vulpes*), the pine marten (*Martes martes*) and the otter (*Lutra lutra*). Red deer (*Cervus elephas*), red squirrel (*Sciurus vulgaris*) and, on a smaller scale, bats (*Chiroptera*) and pigmy shrews (*Sorex minutus*) would have been likely prey species but rats (*Rattus*), mice and possibly also hedgehogs (*Erinaceus europaeus*) would not have appeared in the Burren until after the coming of man.

The natural history of the Burren's vegetation

Though there is some debate over detail it is widely accepted that the slow-motion advance and retreat of the ice over the duration of the Pleistocene (Ice Age) explains how some of the Burren's remarkable flora originally got there. Seeds of arctic plants held up in the boulder clay beneath the ice or mixed up in the particulate debris within were transported from location to location. Most would not have survived the extreme conditions but a few would have been sufficient to facilitate their spread. In the periods of ice retreat, during the interstadials, southern-based plants would have spread northwards to occupy the freshly 'rotovated' ground more or less free from competition.

There is little doubt, though, that the final advance of the ice 11,000-10,000 years ago must have eradicated such southern plants from the Burren. They may have survived in parts of the south of Ireland which were not overrun by the final advance. A northward spread could then have occurred during the post-glacial amelioration. Though admittedly simplistic, it is difficult without having recourse to an explanation of this kind to account for the origins of the remarkable mixture of arctic, montane and Mediterranean flora to be found amid the Atlantic plant communities of the present-day Burren. Explanations which suggest the involvement of migrating birds, animals or indeed humans do not have the same ring of plausibility, though one or other may have been minor, subsidiary agencies. The pollen of that well-known arctic-alpine, the mountain avens (*Dryas*) has been found in the north and west of Ireland dating from tens of thousands of years ago – long before the end of the Ice Age. It is easy to imagine it surviving on isolated nunataks (rocky outcrops above the ice) and through insect pollination being dispersed to more expansive rocky regions where suitable ground conditions prevailed.

With the scouring action of the ice on the Burren uplands, the deposition of till cannot have been substantial except in the valleys. Immediately after the ice retreat there was a protracted period of meltwater action which would have washed clean many of the ice-shaped hill shoulders and removed much of the material into the crevices. More would have become superimposed on the drift already filling the valley floors: hillwash material. Some of this post-glacial material has even been found underground on the floors of the Burren's caves.

The Irish hare, *Lepus timidus hibernicus*.

Man (and his animals) may well have had an effect on the distribution of soil cover in the Burren at a later stage but he cannot be identified with, for instance, soilless areas of limestone pavement which have glacially rounded boulders lying directly on them – obviously in exactly the positions where they were deposited by the retreating ice.

Vegetation Cover of the Burren since the Ice Age

(Simplified diagram based on the pollen diagrams of Watts, Crabtree *et al.*)

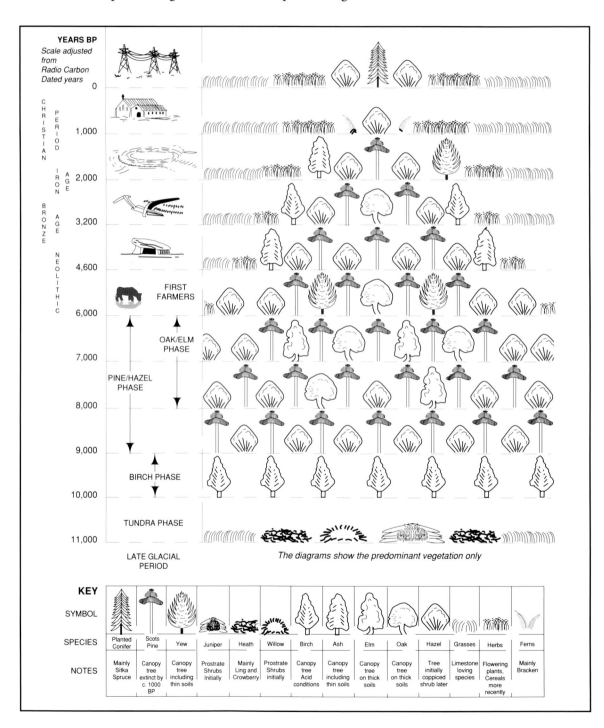

The closed depression at Carron has been described geologically as a polje – a large valley-like basin in the limestone which was formed originally in pre-glacial times. It was, however, extensively shaped into a gentle U valley during the Ice Age and today contains the largest of the Burren's turloughs. Borehole investigation carried out in the turlough bed has shown that it was a permanent lake at the end of the Ice Age. Peat deposits in the substrate have enabled a pollen analysis to be carried out which, though not precisely dated, certainly demonstrates the arboreal succession which must have existed in the Burren uplands in the post-glacial period. Initially birch dominated but was soon replaced by pine and hazel. Oak, elm, ash and alder spread into the area later but never formed a climax woodland on the uplands (as they did elsewhere in the lowlands).

This forest succession has been corroborated by a number of pollen cores taken from wetland locations in the south-eastern edge of the Burren. Dating has further clarified the situation. Lakes in the area of Rinn na Mona and Gortlecka, beneath Mullaghmore were particularly revealing. Pollen from plants growing in the vicinity had accumulated in the brown algal muds in the lake beds. Pollen analysis from a very small lake in this vicinity showed pine, juniper, and hazel to be dominant early colonizers, with birch having a significant phase in the early post-glacial period. Elm and oak peaked about 6,500 years ago, though their presence was significant almost throughout. Alder had a corresponding, though weaker, trace. Ash and yew did not appear until about 6,000 years ago and were significant only until early Christian times. Pollen of species like guelder rose indicated variety in the shrub layer. Bracken and ling showed to a minor degree and suggested heathy cover on the hills, possibly in association with conifers.

Despite the fact that pollen depositions can be misleading in that some plants produce more than others and that some like Scots pine can travel widely on the wind, there can be little

Mountain avens.

doubt that these cores indicate a generally wooded Burren with open country only where soil was sparse or non-existent. It was in these bare or thinly soil-covered patches that the flora which is so typical of the Burren today managed to survive. Forest invasion would have precluded survival of most elements of the flora elsewhere for they would have been out-competed by the trees or the ground storey plants beneath.

Ballymihil Cave (near Poulnabrone in the heart of the region) has revealed woodland snails and hardwood charcoal within its post-glacial sediments indicating heavily wooded conditions. It is likely that the upper ground was largely conifer-covered while the valleys were filled with hardwood forest, from about 2,000 years after the end of the Ice Age. Post-glacial remains in Newhall and Edenvale caves have revealed the presence of birds like the jay (*Garrulus glandarius*), the hawfinch (*Coccothraustes c.*) and the great-spotted woodpecker (*Dendrocopus major*). These are all woodland species and further reinforce the heavily wooded scenario. (Of the three only the jay remains as a resident in Irish woods today!) The remains of goshawk (*Accipiter gentilis*) and capercaillie (*Tetrao urogallus*) have been exposed at the Mesolithic settlement of Mount Sandel in the north of Ireland. These were climax woodland birds and the first men to arrive in the Burren may well have encountered them too.

Early man and the Burren

The archaeological evidence suggests that the first human hunter-gatherers came along the coast, for their kitchen middens (eating places) have been found at a number of places along the Munster coastline. The refuse from their feasts has shown that they ate large quantities of oysters and other shellfish and that they caught and ate the now extinct, flightless, great auk (*Alca impennis*). Ancient kitchen middens of this kind were found at Lahinch, Fisherstreet, and in the dunes at Fanore. A good number of **fulachta fiadha**, which were prehistoric open-air cooking places, are known around the Burren (as, for instance, adjacent to Gleninagh Castle). Tradition links these cooking sites with the activities of nomadic hunting people like the Fianna. Very few have been excavated to date and if we are to find out more about the early fauna of the Burren, these would be worth excavating for traces.

The influence of the arrival of the first farmers to the Burren in the early Neolithic (about 5,000 years ago) can be interpreted from the pollen record. Grasses, plantain and cereals can all be seen to increase noticeably in the pollen diagrams showing the effect that they had on the land. There is a corresponding fall-off in tree pollen reflective of the felling and clearing programme embarked upon by these industrious farmers. Judging from the wealth of Neolithic and Bronze Age archaeological remains (mostly in the form of tombs) the population increased fairly steadily in that period, aided no doubt by the good grazing on the thin soils of the Burren hills and the ease with which the pines and hazel could be removed to create new grazing land. Investigations carried out in the Burren caves have shown that by 3,000-4,000 years ago (early Bronze Age) there had been substantial soil loss from the limestone uplands. Could this have been the result of upland tree clearance followed by overgrazing? These pre-Christian farmers had livestock mainly in the form of goats and cattle. The latter required fair pasture but the former, being capable of eating almost anything growing, could survive in the wilder uplands. Goats must have had a significant influence on the containment of the shrub layer and in ensuring that trees, once felled, did not easily regenerate.

It is difficult now to develop a picture of what conditions were like in those times: weather conditions would seem to have been generally favourable to agricultural activities. It is tempting to assume that precipitation was high given the quantities of soil washed into underground caves at this time. A clue that perhaps the climate then was warmer than it is today exists in the traces of the sub-aquatic water plants *Naias marina* (now absent from Ireland) dating from the time of the early farmers at Gortlecka, in the Burren.

Archaeology, besides being a repository of knowledge about how our forefathers lived must also be regarded as a key to secrets about past wildlife. In the excavation of sites, bones, antlers, artefacts made from animal products or stylised animal replicas are often uncovered, indicating the wild and domestic fauna of the time. They often show as well how man exploited these animals as a food source. The science of archaeo-zoology has developed to such an extent that it is possible (from the bones) to establish livestock species, methods of husbandry and even predominant animal diseases from thousands of years ago. The Burren has yet to be comprehensively investigated by archaeologists but there are plans to do so in the not-too-distant future. Exciting and thought-provoking finds have already been found at the few sites excavated to date. An ornament manufactured from a boar tusk and dating from about 4,000 years ago was found at Poulawack – a clue perhaps to the role wild animals played in Bronze Age art. Excavations at the **fulacht fiadh** at Fahee South, Carron have revealed butchery remnants from about 3,000 years ago. They included both domestic (cattle, horse) and wild (red deer) remains. Chop-marks on deer antlers found would suggest that fragments

A **fulacht fiadh** adjacent to Gleninagh Castle.

were taken at the site for working into tools or artefacts later. Who knows what this area of investigation might reveal in time to come.

Despite the tree clearances that were going on in the Burren in the Bronze Age it can never have been so widespread an activity as to have rendered large tracts treeless. Regardless of whether or not it was within his capabilities, it would have been self-defeating for Bronze Age man to have completely removed the habitat of large huntable mammals like wild boar and red deer. It is likely that in the Burren (as elsewhere in the country) large forests remained, particularly around the edges, well into Christian times.

Cahercommaun cliff fort, near Carron was excavated by archaeologists from Harvard

University in 1934. The site was dated to the ninth century AD and was found to contain abundant domestic animal bones comprising 97 per cent cattle, 1 per cent pig, 1 per cent sheep and goats. The remaining 1 per cent contained the bones of wild animals and included animals found there today like fox, badger and pine marten. Red deer bones found at the site would suggest a more arboreal landscape than at present.

The majority of the stone-built ring forts or cahers (of which more than 400 still exist in the Burren) are thought to date from early Christian times. The ancient annals suggest that internecine feuding was endemic and probably is the main reason why they were so heavily protected. It is a fact also that cattle were secured within the outer enclosures at night to protect them from wolves. It is not known how long wolves survived in the Burren but they probably did so even after most of the woodlands were removed. As long as wild or ill-protected ungulates remained there would be wolves. Considering they managed to survive into the late eighteenth century elsewhere in Ireland it is very likely that there were wolves in the Burren in post-medieval times.

Natural history in the place–names

The old Irish place-names can be indicative of the flora and fauna of a particular locality. It is difficult now to ascribe a definite chronology to these names but many can be traced back to early Christian times and some are decidedly more ancient. The com-

Above: a stone-built ring fort viewed from the air.

Left: feral goat herd below Slieve Carran.

BOX 1

Agriculture in the Burren – Historic Records

c 900 AD
Despite the small quantity (less than 1 per cent) of sheep remains uncovered in excavations at Cahercommaun it is thought that sheep rearing may have been an important agricultural activity in the Burren in early Christian times. Artefacts associated with spinning, weaving and associated industry were found which would suggest both the widespread husbandry of sheep and the organised processing of their wool in the region at that time.

c 1800 AD
'Burrin' This barony is extremely rocky, but provides a short sweet herbage fit for sheep of middling size and short clothing wool, of which immense numbers are annually reared, and usually sold at the fair at Ballinasloe in October and from thince drove into Leinster to be fattened at 3 years old; a small part feeds store bullocks and a much smaller fattens them for Limerick or Cork market. The herbage produced in those of the best quality is of the most nutritive kind, and plentifully intermixed with yarrow, white clover, trefoil, bird's foot trefoil and fattens a few black cattle and immense flocks of sheep, the mutton of which is among the best in Ireland.'
'Potatoes, oats, wheat, barley and flax are grown on cultivated parts (only a small percentage of the area is under tillage)'.
'In those vast tracts of rocky ground in Burren devoted almost exclusively to the rearing of sheep the use of hay is almost unknown. In this part of the country the graziers are very much in the practice of permitting their summer grass to remain untouched until the following spring; it is here called winterage'.

Extracts from statistical survey of County Clare, Dutton (1808).

mon Irish name for the wolf is **bреαch** and a wolf haunt (or the place, perhaps where one was killed) is **bреαch-mhαgh**. In County Clare it occurs in about eight places as breaghva or in one case as breaffy. **Mαc-tíре**, is another ancient name for the wolf. This is the origin of the place name Knockaunvicteera (the little hill of the wolf) just outside Lisdoonvarna.

Horses have obviously been kept in the Burren for centuries as place names testify. Slievenagry near Kilfenora is mentioned in the Annals of the Four Masters where it is Slieve-na-ngroigheadh (the mountain of the horses) and Slieve-na-gcapall near Bell Harbour is suggestive of the same (Joyce, 1901).

A line in one of the Dindshennachus poems from the ninth century refers to the Burren – **Da ðhαmh αllαíðh α Boíрínn** – 'two wild oxen from the Burren' (transl. O'Curry). This was part of a ransom required by Cormac to redeem his chief at Tara and it suggests how well known the Burren was as an agricultural region in those days. The abundance of cattle bones from Cahercommaun would tend to substantiate this.

Many other animals are mentioned in the Burren place-names like Muckinish (the isle of the pigs); Lios na Gcat (the fort of the cat or pine marten); Carrow na Maddra (the marsh of the dog or fox). The deer park associated with Lemeaneh castle is more likely to have held introduced fallow deer than the native red deer as the former was widely kept for venison in medieval estate enclosures.

Burren place-names also refer to birds as in Keelhilla, a corrupt form of 'the wood of the eagle', appropriately beneath Eagle's Rock on Slieve Carran. Both the wood and the eagle are now gone but the place-name remains to tell of a time when this raptor nested on the cliff-face and hunted in the woodland below. The bones of the white-tailed eagle (*Haliaeetus albicilla*) were found at Cahercommaun and it was known to have nested at the cliffs of Moher until the 1840s, suggesting an occupation of the Burren for a thousand years at least.

Finds of crane (*Grus grus*) bones from the Ennis caves show that this stately bird, which was widely known in the Irish boglands until the Middle Ages was also found in the Clare wetlands. There is a possibility that it inhabited the extensive wetlands along the south-eastern boundary of the Burren where the bittern (*Botaurus stellaris*), another extinct Irish bird, may also have been found. The latter was often on sale at the Ennis market in the early nineteenth century (Thompson, 1850). In the excavation of a crannog in Ballyalla lake, north of Ennis, the bones of many wetland birds were uncovered, dating from pre-medieval times. A dozen species of waterfowl were identified including both diving and surface-feeding ducks and geese, and great-crested (*Podiceps cristatus*) and little grebes (*Tachybaptus ruficollis*). Wading birds were represented by golden plover (*Pluvialis apricaria*), snipe (*Gallinago g.*), grey heron (*Ardea cinerea*) and others. These birds were captured and eaten by the crannog-dwellers and, interestingly, all those mentioned are still to be found at Ballyalla lake today (the name itself means the townland of the swans).

Indicative as they may be of individual birds and animals, place-names are most illustrative in the case of plants and of past landscapes. Wetlands, for instance, are recorded in Irish words such as **рíαsc, monα, turlαch** and **léαnα**, sometimes long after the wetland has disappeared through drainage. Each can be suggestive of a specific kind of wetland or of a dominant type of vegetation. **Seíscεαnn**, for example means a sedgy place (from **seísc**, sedge). There are references in the Burren place-names to specific dryland plants: Creevagh alludes to a place where wild garlic was common, and Rannagh means a ferny place. Both are ground-storey plants often associated with deciduous woods. It is thus reasonable to deduce that in each of these localities (now devoid of garlic, at any rate) there were once deciduous woodlands. There are many place-names referring to now-vanished woodlands and suggesting more widespread treescapes even in historical times. While Slieve Callan (mountain of the hazels) is still hazel-clad in places, Behagh (the place of the birches) near Abbey Hill, Derrynavahagh (the oak wood of the birches) and Feenagh (a wooded place), are now completely treeless. Behagh may have been part of the wood of Siudaine which sheltered Conor O'Brien in the thirteenth century and which mantled the slopes of the north-facing hills, in the vicinity of Corcomroe. A number of place-names refer to oak woods on the western side of the Burren: oak trees are nowadays virtually non-existent throughout the region.

In all the many place-names which help our perception of how the Burren once looked and of the plant communities which dominated in different parts, there is an apparent total lack of reference to the remarkable floral communities of the open limestone today. Could this be as a result of the names having been lost in the course of history or is it possible that these floral displays were restricted to smaller, less noticable patches when place-names were becoming established? We can be fairly sure that woodland cover was, even within historical times, much more widespread than at present, but it is hard to believe that the colourful and visually descriptive language from which these place-names sprang would have ignored or overlooked even small patches of brightly coloured and unusual plants. This anomoly is compounded by the paucity or complete absence of the pollen of the more unusual of the Burren flowers. Although evidence of shrubby cinquefoil (*Potentilla fruticosa*) can be traced back perhaps a thousand years and rock-rose (*Helianthemum*) and mountain avens to post-glacial and glacial times respectively, there is no ancient pollen of that ubiquitous Burren beauty the spring gentian (*Gentiana verna*). None the less, there can be no doubt about the ancient lineage of this flora and perhaps with the more intensive investigation which will surely accompany the archaeological work, additional light will be cast upon this and others of the Burren's many enigmas.

Habitats

A Variety of Environments

From a distance the Burren landscape gives the impression of uniformity. This is especially true of the view from the coastline of Connemara, on the north side of Galway Bay. It has the appearance of a low, rather featureless, plateau which slopes to the sea in a series of step-like terraces. Along the eastern boundary the landscape looks similar but the plateau terminates more irregularly at Mullaghmore in a series of conspicuous folds. Only along the southern perimeter is it ill-defined topographically. Here the limestone disappears beneath the younger shales but at roughly the same ground level. The boundary can be located without difficulty, however, due to the markedly different rushy vegetation which grows on the poorly drained soils overlying the shales.

A glimpse of a prehistoric habitat: Scots pines against the terraced hillside.

The Topography of The Burren

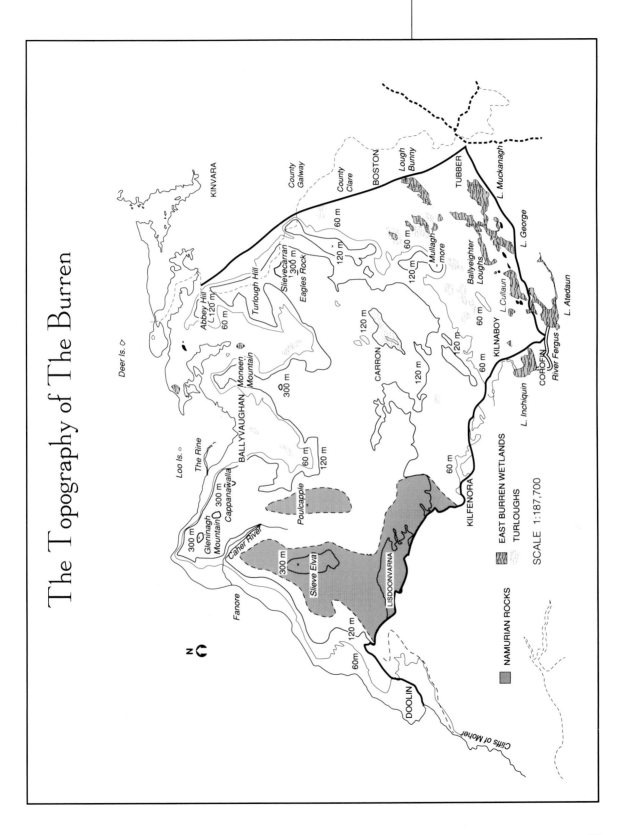

KINVARA

County
Galway

County
Clare

BOSTON

Lough
Bunny

TUBBER

L. Muckanagh

60 m

L. George

Slievecarran
300 m

Eagles Rock

Turlough Hill

Ballyeighter
Loughs

Mullaghmore

120 m

120 m

60 m

60 m

120 m

Abbey Hill
L. 120 m

60 m

Deer Is.

Moneen
Mountain

300 m

CARRON

120 m

120 m

L. Cullaun

KILNABOY

20 m

60 m

COROFIN

River Fergus

L. Atedaun

Loo Is.

The Rine

BALLYVAUGHAN

Cappanawalla

300 m

60 m

120 m

L. Inchiquin

60 m

Gleninagh
Mountain

300 m

Caher River

Poulcapple

KILFENORA

EAST BURREN WETLANDS

300 m

Slieve Elva

LISDOONVARNA

TURLOUGHS

SCALE 1:187,700

Fanore

120 m

NAMURIAN ROCKS

N

60m

DOOLIN

Cliffs of Moher

Despite the overview, however the Burren is far from uniform. It is a complex of dry lime-stone habitats, freshwater wetlands, woodlands, scrublands, grasslands and a varied coastline. The dry limestone itself can be subdivided into lowlands, slopes and escarpments and uplands. At mainly below 300 metres (1,000 feet) the uplands are hills rather than mountains and much is plateau.

The wetlands comprise turloughs, cut-away bog, lakes, fens and combinations of these. With the exception of the Caher River there is very little flowing surface water in the region. There is some cut-away fen in the south-east and some intact blanket bog on one or two of the mountains. The coastline, though mainly rocky along its length, has inter-esting variations in the dune sys-tem at Fanore, the Rine saltmarsh and the inlets and is-lets of south Galway Bay.

Freshwater wetlands.

While the coastline and to a large extent the wetlands are 'natural' in that they have hardly been modified by man, the Burren proper has been modified repeatedly, to the extent that it is mostly 'semi-natural' and large sectors are being actively farmed as agricultural land. The areas most utilised in this manner are in the drift-filled valleys and in isolated solution hollows where soil has accumulated, but even on the slopes and uplands patches have been cleared for agriculture, particularly since the 1970s.

The imprint of man's past on the Burren landscape

Despite the fact that there has been human settlement in the Burren for at least 5,000 years, the landscape remains relatively unspoiled. Man-modification in the form of tree removal followed by substantial soil removal (as outlined in 'Burren Beginnings') has certainly changed the Burren and its habitats but the landscape has accommodated quietly to these changes. Even the memorials to the dead, the dolmens, cists and cairns, are entirely in keeping with the rocky topography.

Aerial photographs have revealed the foundations of dozens of circular habitations on the top of Turlough Hill. These may have been temporary dwellings of valley people who retired to the immense pre-Christian enclosure on the mountain top as a seasonal aspect of their lifestyle. Their rituals and culture are now lost but the site still radiates pagan mystery. The enclosure overlooks the early Christian settlement at Oughtmama and the later monastic settlement at Corcomroe. Land terracing and ancient field boundaries show clearly that these ascetics were capable of prodigious feats in working the land.

The lazy beds, relief roads and deserted cottages are man-made relics of a time when the Burren was populated by a burgeoning peasantry, particularly on the better land along the coastal fringes. Sea fisheries, which had been in operation along this coastline (as elsewhere around the Irish coast) since time immemorial, failed to sustain a stricken people who were highly dependent on subsistance farming. Large-scale depopulation through famine and emigration resulted, which leaves the Burren today, a century and a half later, one of the least populated regions of the country.

Derelict but not deserted: abandoned by man but welcomed by nature.

But while agriculture was failing, technology was succeed-

BOX 2

Land use in the Burren

The primary uses of the Burren are for agricultural purposes and for forestry. The areas under consideration are Ballyvaughan and Corofin DEDs, (District Electoral Divisions) 62,500 hectares (153,000 acres)

Agriculture Primary land uses: grassland and livestock.
(a) Beef cattle rearing and fattening (low output/low input system).
(b) Dairying (presently a minority enterprise and not in areas of ecological interest).
(c) Sheep rearing (has not been an important enterprise in the Burren for centuries)
(d) Tillage was traditionally practised in the drift district of the north-east is now almost non-existent in the region.
(e) Silage is now the major crop in the areas containing thicker soils.

In *1989 there were*:   36,800 cattle,
                          4,800 dairying beasts
                          16,000 sheep

Land usage for livestock is generally 4.3 acres/livestock unit (good land) and 8.0 acres/livestock unit (Slieve Elva district). Overall the livestock statistic is probably about 2 acres/livestock unit.

Forestry Planting was carried out in the 1960s and 1970s on the shale outliers north of Lisdoonvarna and near Noughval. An area of 1,700 hectares (4,250 acres) is presently under timber comprising approximately 95 per cent sikta spruce; 3 per cent lodgepole pine; 1 per cent larch; 1 per cent broadleaves.

A substantial programme of further planting (about 50hectares per annum) is planned for the mid-Clare region (south of the Burren) over the next few years.

ing in making inroads into the region. Mining for minerals like fluorspar and calcite and for metals such as zinc, lead and silver were opening up the Burren to modern exploitation. The landscape managed to survive these mainly abortive ravages and offers them today both as testimony to man's endeavour and also as interesting man-made habitats.

Though the population density of the Burren proper is presently one of the lowest in Ireland, as many as 50 per cent of its 3,300 or so residents are involved in agriculture. An extensive (as opposed to an intensive) system of agriculture is practiced. Traditionally the Burren is famous for its winterages where a kind of 'reverse booleying' is practised - because of the availability of winter grazing, livestock are taken up to the high ground for that period and removed to the lowlands again in spring. Cattle are by far the most important livestock species with some 40,000 head in 2,000 herds. Only half as many sheep are herded, mainly in richer valleys, but with recent EC grants and increased headage payments their numbers have been growing rapidly in recent years. A considerable number of feral goats roam the uplands in a semi-wild state: with their catholic appetites they have a significant effect on the distribution of plants like hazel scrub. Silage and hay are the main crops with a noticeable increase in the former (and decrease in the latter) since 1986. Traditionally, artifical fertiliser has not been part of the agricultural regime in the Burren, but with increasing silage acreage, applications like slurry have become more commonplace.

Tillage, which has been decreasing steadily for decades is now almost non-existent in the Burren. The rich land of the northern coastal strip in the vicinity of Finavarra was traditional tillage land and some fodder crops are still grown there.

Forestry is localised in the Burren region. Large plantations exist on Slieve Elva (arguably, however, this is not part of the true Burren) and to the west of corkscrew hill with smaller blocks between Noughaval and Lisdoonvarna. The main species are Sitka spruce (*Picea sitchensis*) with some lodgepole pine (*Pinus contorta*) though there are minor stands of larch (*Larix*) and hardwoods in places.

Lowland Habitats

Excluding the drift-mantled coastal fringe and valleys to the north the Burren lowlands are mainly uncultivated rocky flatlands. Along the eastern boundary and widening out into the extensive Gort lowlands of south-west Galway, they exist in a surface-shattered or fragmented form composed of irregular chunks of weathered, fossiliferous limestone. Along the western side and outcropping on the terraces at higher levels the limestone is smoother and exists in discrete clints (slabs) and grikes (crevices). Though patches of this 'pavement' exist throughout the region, the majority of the lowland flats are of the surface-shattered type. Locally, steep-sided hollows (dolines) are common features. In the south-west they are so distinctive as to create a two-tiered topography. The lowlands are liberally criss-crossed with dry-stone walls but are in some places quite open – usually where there is an associated wetland.

The valleys are floored with glacial drift (mainly boulder clay) with accumulations of hillwash from the valley sides and in the deeper hollows. Over most of the lowlands soils are very thin, patchy or non-existent. They are classified as rendzinas (thin, well-drained, organic, brown earths) and are highly productive. Limestone grassland is the predominant vegetation of the rendzinas though it is not confined to the lowlands and grows on the terraces at higher altitudes.

Because of the regional variation of the lowland habitats no attempt has been made to generalise their particular natural characteristics. Rather, two widely separate locations at similar altitudes above sea level have been compared.

The 200 hectare (500-acre) Ballyryan district in the south west is generally regarded as one of the most ecologically interesting in the entire Burren: it is regarded as being of international importance. 'Many of the most characteristic [plant] communities of the Burren are found here and the ecological interest is further enhanced by the admixture of marine plants into the arctic and alpine groups that are also found elsewhere.' (An Foras Forbartha Report, 1972). The complexity of the structure of the plant communities in these lowland situations was demonstrated by Ivimey-Cook and Proctor (1966), who identified no less than ten plant associations varying with a range of environmental factors between Ballyryan and the sea.

Near the sea the grassland communities are dominated by

Limestone grassland in typical lowland setting

ten or so coastal species such as sea pink (*Armeria maritima*) and bladder campion (*Silene vulgaris*). Beyond the normal influence of the sea spray bird's foot trefoil (*Lotus corniculatus*) and purging flax (*Linum catharticum*) are in evidence with spring sandwort (*Minuartia verna*), harebell (*Campanula rotundifolia*), wild thyme (*Thymus serpyllum*), cudweed (*Filago vulgaris*), squinancywort

(*Asperula cynanchica*) and others. Further back still, and slightly higher, and the lowland flora becomes fully developed. It includes mountain avens (*Dryas octopetala*), bloody cranesbill (*Geranium sanguineum*), hoary rock-rose (*Helianthemum canum*), hairy rockcress (*Arabis hirsuta*), field stitchwort (*Stellaria holostea*), kidney vetch (*Anthyllis vulneraria*), stone bramble (*Rubus saxatilis*), salad burnet (*Sanguisorba minor*), spring gentian (*Gentiana verna*), eyebright (*Euphrasia* spp.) and a varity of others, less dominant.

Shrubby vegetation dominates in the hollows where there is shelter and more soil and includes hazel, holly, and ash with whitethorn (*Crataegus monogyna*) and blackthorn (*Prunus spinosa*). Occasional buckthorn (*Rhamnus catharticus*), whitebeam (*Sorbus aria*) and dogwood (*Cornus sanguinea*) are found there too. The flora of these hollows is noticably is less diverse than that found on the adjacent limestone grasslands.

The invertebrate fauna of the Ballyryan area is also most interesting. Two Lusitanian species (species with south-west European affinities) have been identified there – one is a woodlouse and the other, a beetle. This is also one of the best locations in the Burren for butterflies and moths, holding many of the scarce and range-limited species. The rare Burren green moth (*Calamia tridens o.*) is found here also.

The birdlife is richest in the summer, supporting nesting meadow pipits (*Anthus pratensis*), skylarks (*Alauda arvensis*), wheatears (*Oenanthe o.*), whitethroats (*Sylvia communis*), stonechats (*Saxicola torquata*) and other passerine (perching) birds.

One of the largest feral goat herds (more than 100 individuals) is usually found in the area. Both badger and fox are known to reside there and it is one of the best locations for pine martens and stoats in the whole Burren region.

The open limestone flatlands at the foot of Mullaghmore and extending towards Lough Bunny are also well studied and are a species-rich habitat. At least 15 recognisable plant communities are to be found at Mullaghmore, seven of which are on dry land. The grassland includes blue moor-grass (*Sesleria albicans*), crested hairgrass (*Koeleria macrantha*) and quaking grass (*Briza media*) among many others. The plant assemblages include; cudweed, squinancywort, mouse-ear hawkweed (*Pilosella pilosellina*), spring and field gentian (*Gentianella campestris*), slender bedstraw (*Galium sterneri*) and several orchid species including fragrant, fly, bee, butterfly, frog and the Mediterannean speciality, the dense-flowered orchid (*Neotinea maculata*) which also grows at altitude in the adjacent hills. Almost all the plants found at Ballyryan (with the exception of the coastal species) are found also at Mullaghmore. At Ballyryan however there tends to be a greater density of some species such as hoary rock-rose.

Investigation of the invertebrates has shown the area to be especially rich. For instance, 20 species of weevils (Curculionidae) have been identified, three rare beetles (one new to Ireland; two new to Clare) and a diversity of butterflies and day-flying moths.

Birds include stonechats, wheatears, whitethroats and other open-country species found elsewhere in the Burren. There are many ecological similarities between the dry limestone flatlands around Mullaghmore and that part of Ballyryan not influenced by the sea, despite the fact that they are on opposite sides of the Burren.

Intermediate Habitats

The Black Head district demonstrates well the lowland to upland limestone habitat profile. From sea level where there are shattered blocks and wave-cut platforms, the limestone slopes gradually upwards to grassy terraces and limestone pavement. Heathy uplands with rock scarps cap the summit at about 300 metres (about 1,000 feet) above sea level. The limestone headland has been rounded off by the action of the last glaciation and a field of glacial boulders lies to the south-west where they were dumped by the retreating ice. The Gleninagh valley to the east of the headland is mantled in glacial drift as are the other valley floors to the south and east.

Lowland to upland limestone habitat profile.

Excluding the salt-resistant coastal plants like sea pink (*Armeria maritima*), bladder campion (*Silene vulgaris*), and sea spleenwort (*Asplenium marinum*), which proliferate on Black Head, the lowland community includes such species as common chickweed (*Stellaria media*), clovers (*Trifolium* spp.), bents (*Agrostis* spp.), fescues (*Festuca* spp.), wall rue (*Asplenium ruta-muraria*), occasional hemp agrimony (*Eupatorium cannabinum*), brooklime (*Veronica beccabunga*) and pearlwort (*Sagina* spp.).

Above the road circuiting the headland, maidenhair fern (*Adiantum capillus-veneris*) is found in the grikes and damp rock recesses. Wood sage (*Teucrium scorodonia*), false brome grass (*Brachypodium sylvaticum*), St John's wort (*Hypericum* spp.) share the habitat. The plant community at and above this level is complex with abundant mountain avens, wild thyme, devil's bit scabious (*Succisa pratensis*), harebell, grasses including sheep's fescue (*Festuca ovina*) and abundant blue moor-grass. Several cushion-type mosses like *Tortella* are also found. Mossy (*Saxifraga hypnoides*) and Irish saxifrage (*Saxifraga rosacea*) grow down to near sea level and are often associated with sea pink and wall pellitory (*Parietaria diffusa*).

Many butterflies and diurnal moths are found in the vicinity of Black Head – notably the small blue (*Cupido minimus*) and the burnet family (Zygaenidae). Lizards (*Lacerta vivipara*) bask in sunny places, out of the wind. Common summer birds include stonechats, wheatears and ravens. Black guillemots (*Cepphus grylle*) nest near the light station. In winter, great northern divers (*Gavia immer*) can be seen regularly off the headland and cetaceans (dolphins and porpoises) are often sighted in warmer weather.

Upland Habitats

This profuse plant diversity gradually reduces with altitude, giving way to heathland comprised mainly of *Calluna*. At about 200 metres (650 feet), bearberry (*Arctostaphylos uva-ursi*) and crowberry (*Empetrum nigrum*), combine with mountain avens and, to a lesser degree, ling to form the upland heath community. In places where peat has developed, ling and bell heather (*Erica cinerea*) dominate with purple moor-grass (*Molinia caerulea*) and juniper.

It is thought that this may be the remnant of former widespread heathland cover. The existence of wintergreen (*Pyrola media*), a ground-storey plant of pinewoods, is suggestive of former native conifer woodland covering these uplands.

In addition to the well-developed upland plant assemblages the area has its fair share of peculiarities including a sandwort (*Arenaria norvegica*) found nowhere else in Ireland (but not seen for 30 years), naturalised cotoneaster (*C. microphyllus*) and others. Plants such as maidenhair fern, hoary rock-rose and dark red helleborine (*Epipactis atrorubens*) are locally common.

Though barely 300 metres (1,000 feet) in altitude, the ridge which runs northwards from Mullaghmore towards Galway Bay has in places a well-developed upland flora. Particularly interesting are the woodland pockets which comprise ash and hazel with hawthorn and some rowan (*Sorbus aucuparia*). Both wych elm (*Ulmus glabra*) and aspen (*Populus tremula*) are found in a natural state-a situation now rare in County Clare. Broad-leaved helleborine (*Epipactis helleborine*), stone bramble, guelder rose (*Viburnum opulus*) and golden rod (*Solidago virgaurea*) form part of the ground community of plants beneath the wood. On the hill slopes heathy plants like mountain avens, ling, heath grasses and heath pea (*Lathyrus montanus*) dominate and in particularly acid locations, bell heather and velvet bent (*Agrostis canina*) are found.

The woodland growing on the face of Slieve Carran is semi-natural. It is predominantly hazel and ash but there are also birch trees, a smaller number of rowan and a few spindle trees (*Euonymus europaeus*). The interesting ground plant cover includes herb robert (*Geranium robertianum*), wild violets (*Viola* spp.), ivy (*Hedera helix*), wood avens (*Geum urbanum*), barren strawberry (*Potentilla sterilis*) and false brome grass with abundant wood sorrel (*Oxalis acetosella*) and bramble (*Rubus fruticosus*). The community also contains wild strawberry (*Fragaria vesca*), cuckoo pint (*Arum maculatum*), wood sedge (*Carex sylvatica*), honeysuckle (*Lonicera periclymenum*) and yellow pimpernel (*Lysimachia nemorum*), along with the scarcer broad-leaved helleborine and heath pea. Mosses and liverworts abound in this habitat.

A restricted Burren flora covers the top of the cliff and extends down a short way. This includes spring sandwort (*Minuartia verna*), heather, mountain avens, sheep's fescue and St John's wort, with hairy rockcress and mossy saxifrage in smaller quantity. Along with the woods of the Glen of Clab (in the central Burren) these small remnants form the best-developed, most natural and consequently most valuable stands in the entire region. There are few ashwoods on limestone in Ireland that are approaching climax forest, so Slieve Carran's woods are ecologically important. It is interesting that the woods grow only on the southern side of the valley and of Poulavallan (a collapse hollow to the west of the Glen of Clab — itself an interesting place), surely a consequence of boulder-clay deposition from southerly moving glaciation. The moss and liverwort communities are of special value with ten rare species.

Ash woodland in the Glen of Clab.

The cliff also has interesting nesting birds including kestrel (*Falco tinnunculus*) raven, and occasionally peregrine (*Falco peregrinus*).

The upland plateau is irregularly covered with the organic brown earths typical of most of the region and supports a similar rich grassland community. Most visitors to the Burren are oblivious of the grasslands of the upper ground, but the practice of cattle winterage on these uplands testifies to their abundance. Investigation of the plant diversity has shown that these grasslands are less species-rich, generally, than their lowland counterparts though many of the dominant species are found throughout. There is a tendency towards heathland where the heavily leached soils are thickest. On the summits of some of the hills heathers, sedges and mosses dominate the grassland community while in other places there is a preponderance of bearberry, juniper and heathy grassland. Not many birds breed in this upland habitat though meadow pipits and skylarks are widespread. Wheatears occur at rocky outcrops and wrens are found in the stone walls. In winter occasional 'trips' of golden plover, and occasional curlews and snipe are found, but the area is generally devoid of avian interest.

The Wetlands

Apart from the east Burren wetlands (which are discussed later) the region, as is to be expected in karstic topography, has little permanent surface water. The Caher river is the only surface-running watercourse: it extends for about 4 kilometres (2.5 miles) before discharging into the sea. It has an abundant and interesting flora which includes rare hybrids of a species of horsetail and of a particular pondweed. The invertebrate fauna is also interesting with abundant larval-stage insect life. Small brown trout (*Salmo trutta*) occur in the river: a fraction develop into sea trout for they are caught regularly at the Fanore outfall. The river supports breeding birds such as grey wagtail (*Motacilla cinerea*) and Irish dipper (*Cinclus cinclus h.*) at one of the only regularly occupied sites in the entire region. Pine martens are well known from the Caher valley. They have been photographed at a breeding site in an abandoned dwelling not far from the river. This unique and isolated valley is, acre for acre, one of the richest locations in the region.

A one kilometre section of river (the Castletown) flows above ground near Carron but it is really an integral part of the Carron turlough. There are many such seasonal lakes in the Burren but that at Carron is by far the largest. When in full winter flood it is approximately 3 kilometres (1.75 miles) long and about half a kilometre (about 500 yards) wide, covering over 150 hectares (350 acres). Geologically it is described as a polje having been formed orginally by the extensive solution of the limestone in the vicinity. Indeed, though it behaves hydrologically like one, it shows

few of the typical turlough characteristics such as a well-defined black moss layer or clearly zoned benthic vegetation. It is notable mainly for its interesting butterflies and other insects and its wildfowl which include wigeon, teal and occasional wild swans and white-fronted geese.

Large turloughs which exhibit typical characteristics exist just to the west of Gort near Garryland. Smaller examples can be seen on the lowlands around Mullaghmore, just south of Ballyvaughan, and of course at Turlough itself, a few kilometres north of Carron village. In the typical turlough the water emerges and retreats through 'swallow holes'. The fluctuating level of water is determined by variations in the ground water table due mainly to increasing rain in winter. Other factors have a bearing too. Caherglassaun turlough in the limestone district south of Kinvara is obviously influenced by tidal fluctuations while some of those at higher altitudes may (contrary to gravitational theory) be more flooded than their lowland counterparts. In the latter case it is thought that complexities of a hydrological nature are responsible.

Carron turlough: left, flooded in winter; below, dry in summer.

Most of the turloughs are fairly shallow, flooding normally to a depth of only a metre or so. In some cases, however the depth may be ten metres (30 feet) or more. Some of the larger lakes like Lough Bunny show characteristics of turloughs in their vegetation and fluctuating watertable. The vegetation exists in discrete bands or zones within the flood basin of the typical turlough. It is typified by two mosses: a blackish one (*Cinclidotus*) which grows only within the limits of long-term flooding; and a robust dark green one (*Fontinalis*) which, being much less tolerant of exposure grows at lower levels. Some flowers such as the violets reflect this characteristic zonation. Plants of the *Potentilla* genus – the shrubby cinquefoil and the silverweed – show water-tolerant characteristics, the former at upper levels of flooding, the latter throughout the turlough bed. The bulbous red-stemmed rush (*Juncus bulbosus*) grows abundantly in many of the Burren's turloughs despite the fact that it normally thrives on acid soil in bogs.

The invertebrate fauna of the turloughs is rich and interesting. Water bugs, beetles, their larvae and the larval stages of others which spend most of their adult lives on the wing abound in turloughs. Certain crustaceans including the fairy shrimp (*Tanymastix stagnalis*), a species unique to turloughs, are also common. Aquatic snails and fish are scarce in true turloughs.

The floating plant seeds and invertebrates are the ingredients of a 'soup' which attracts flocks of wildfowl in winter. Surface-feeding ducks like wigeon and teal are the commonest species.

The east Burren wetland habitats

This system of freshwater wetlands acts as a catchment for much of the uplands of the eastern Burren. It outfalls into the river Fergus at Corofin. Lying between Corofin and Boston it comprises a complex of lakes, turloughs, fens, and cut-away fen. The main entities are (from Corofin): Lough Inchiquin, Lough Atedaun, Lough Cullaun, Lough George, the Ballyeighter Loughs (upper and lower), Lough Muckanagh and Lough Bunny. The total area is in excess of 2,500 hectares (6,150 acres).

Though the system lies mainly in well-drained limestone country with rendzina-type light soils it is nevertheless characterised by impeded drainage. Drainage activities since the mid-nine-

teenth century have connected several of the wetlands and have undoubtedly reduced the extent and duration of flooding.

In general, the major lakes lie at either end of the system, with most of the fen and marsh between. Loughs Bunny, George and Muckanagh are limestone lakes flanked by pavement and partially fringed by fen. Inchiquin and Atedaun are lakes in the glacially formed depressions in the drift over-

BOX 3

The east Burren wetlands

This system of freshwater wetlands extends for some 15 kilometres (9.5 miles) along the south-eastern boundary of the Burren (extending approximately from Boston to Corofin). They are one of the most extensive systems of calcareous wetlands in Ireland. They include the following lakes, fens and turloughs:

Lough Bunny	(Calcareous lake)	195 ha
Ballyeighter Lough (upper)	(Calcareous lake)	232 ha
Ballyeighter Lough (lower)	(Fenny lake)	165 ha
Muckanagh Lough	(Calcareous lake)	670 ha
Lough George	(Calcareous lake)	316 ha
Lough Cullaun	(Calcareous lake)	445 ha
Lough Atedaun	(lake/turlough)	338 ha
Lough Inchiquin	(lake)	166 ha

lying the limestone. The Ballyeighter Loughs lie in extensive flatlands of cut-away fen peat. Several hundred acres of fenland supporting reed beds are a feature of the unworked sections which are subject to shallow flooding.

Despite its vastness, the fenland has to date revealed little of major botanical interest. The ecological importance centres mainly on its invertebrates and birdlife. Both Loughs Atedaun and Bunny were found to be of national botanical importance as a result of field studies carried out by the Wildlife Service, while the remainder of the wetland system was found to be either regionally or locally so.

The vegetation of the wetlands is complex, depending to a large degree on whether local characteristics are mainly those of lakeland, turlough, fen, marsh or bog. The deeper lakes (Inchiquin and Bunny) have deep-water aquatic vegetation and typical emergent vegetation at the edges. Bunny, which is 195 hectares (480 acres) was formed originally by the local-ised collapse of the bedrock. It is the deepest in the system but has shallow edges with complex and varied plant communities. Inchiquin, being entirely in drift,

Facing page: Ancient tree roots at Lough Cullaun in the east Burren wetlands.

Below: Fen vegetation at Lough Bunny.

supports less botanical variation. The vegetation of Lough Bunny deserves special mention, for though it supports many of the wetland plants found throughout the system it has many specialities and rarities besides. Two main fen communities exist one of which is dominated by the sedges *Carex elata, C. lasiocarpa, C. panicea* and *C. demissa*. The other is dominated by the rush *Juncus subnodulosus*, with *Carex nigra*, bog bean (*Menyanthes trifoliata*), spike-rush (*Eleocharis* spp.) and others. Many of the region's orchid species are found in proximity to the lake, including the insect-mimicking fly and bee orchids (*Ophrys* spp.). Dropwort (*Filipendula vulgaris*), which is unknown elsewhere in Ireland, has its centre of distribution near Lough Bunny.

The invertebrate fauna of Lough Bunny is diverse and includes a variety of water snails. A local species, *Aplexa hypnorum*, occurs in the lake. Water bugs have been used as wetland indicator species to investigate the ecology of the lake.

Small numbers of wildfowl of more than a dozen species come to Lough Bunny in the winter months. At least three, mallard, tufted duck and red-breasted merganser, stay to breed in most years. A number of other waterbirds including great crested and little grebe, coot, moorhen and four or five species of wading birds also nest. A colony of some 300 pairs of black-headed gulls (*Larus ridibundus*) breeds annually on one of the lake's islands.

Coastal Habitats

The Burren coastline extends from Doolin in the south-west northwards to Black Head and eastwards to Deer Island and Aughinish. South of the outfall of the Aille River the bedrock changes suddenly from limestone to Namurian shale. East of Aughinish (at the border between County Clare and County Galway) is inner Galway Bay. Although the Cliffs of Moher are beyond our brief they are alluded to elsewhere in the text mainly in regard to their exceptional seabird colonies. The limestone cliffs along the Burren's coastline are nowhere higher than 30 metres (100 feet) and consequently lack the type of habitat provided by, for instance, the limestone cliffs and stacks of Inishmore, in the Aran Islands. There are, nevertheless, low cliffs just north of Doolin and around Black Head.

Elsewhere the limestone meets the sea in a rather benign, irregular manner, most of the heavy erosional work having been carried out by glacial action during the Ice Age. This glacial shaping is evident in the rounding off of the headland at Black Head and in the boulder-strewn pavement on the seaward side of the coast road, north of Fanore. Glacial erratics of Connemara granite occur on the shore at Finavarra. The drift on the Rine peninsula, exposed by wave action, also has glacial origins while the accumulations of cobble-sized, wave-rounded stones on the shore at Gleninagh have occurred in the interim. These beach accumulations have impounded small brackish lakes at Aughinish and at Finavarra (Lough Murree), the latter of which is an important habitat in its own right. Carrickadda, on the seaward side of Lough Murree is an extensive limestone terrace with a rich marine fauna. Illaunloo (Loo Island), a tiny limestone outcrop, lies in Ballyvaughan Bay, about a mile due west of Finavarra point. An area encompassing Carrickadda, Lough Murree and Illaunloo has been designated an Area of Special Scientific Interest in view of its exceptional marine wildlife. Deer Island at the edge of the region is also an important wildlife station.

An extensive sand dune system exists at Fanore and to a minor degree at Bishop's Quarter near Ballyvaughan. Owing to the removal of sand by the wind, the Fanore dunes are partially mobile, revealing glacial features beneath. They have an impressive flora and are regarded as regionally important.

Muddy inlets with saltmarsh exist behind the Rine Point and around Ballyvaughan. A long finger inlet extends into Bell Harbour and reaches Muckinish and Poulnaclough Bays. The coastal wetland habitats hold significant wintering wildfowl and waders and have interesting saltmarsh flora.

In contrast to the variety of habitats along the north Burren coastline, the western seaboard offers relative uniformity. With the exception of the dune system at Fanore it is, in the main, less interesting.

The rocky coastline

At low spring tides a good deal of the rich marine life inhabiting the rocky coastline is exposed. Waving fronds of kelp (*Laminaria*) break the water surface, their stipes firmly attached to the irregular limestone surface. This irregularity is, in places, the consequence of excavations carried out by sea urchins to make their cup-shaped sanctuaries in the rock. Colonies of the purple urchin (*Paracentrotus*) exist along the Burren's rocky coastline particularly between Doolin and Black Head but like most of the marine life are only visible at low tide. Beautiful red and green anemones (*Actinaria*) and a variety of molluscs and crustaceans share the habitat with the urchins. The rock pools abound with barnacles (*Cirripedia*), limpets (*Patella*) and dog whelks (*Nucella lapillus*). Tidal zonation is demonstrated by a range of periwinkles which inhabit different levels, reflecting their degree of tolerance to exposure.

Lichen zonation is also a feature of the rocky coastline and the colour succession of black to yellow to white and grey from below high tide mark to well above it is noticeable in most places. The black *Verrucaria* looks rather like a film of tar on the rock surface but is in fact a salt resistant crustose lichen. The mustard-coloured *Caloplaca* lichen exists in the form of a distinct zone at or around high tide mark but above it forms circular patches. Here the grey-green lichen zone dominates. An extremely rich assemblage of lichens is found on the granite erratics at Finavarra. Dominant flowers of the rocky coast are the sea pink (*Armeria*

Eroded limestone encrusted with barnacles, mussels and dog whelks.

maritima) and the bladder campion (*Silene vulgaris*) which form luxuriant cushions even down to the salt spray zone. In the crevices and grikes grows the fern sea spleenwort (*Asplenium marinum*).

Rock pipits (*Anthus spinoletta*) are common residents of the rocky coast. Turnstones (*Arenaria interpres*) and occasional purple sandpipers (*Calidris maritima*) are also found here, mainly in winter. A few pairs of black guillemots (*Cepphus grylle*) breed in holes in the rocky cliffs at Black Head.

Loo and Deer Island

Both of these islands are interesting habitats but for different species. Loo island (Illaunloo) is a limestone outcrop at the mouth of Ballyvaughan Bay. At spring tides it is virtually completely covered by the sea and is constantly wave-washed. Consquently, the flora comprises marine algae, notably wracks. It is important as a haul-up for common seals (up to 100) and as a pupping station for them in spring and early summer.

Deer Island has a surface area of about 0.2 hectares (0.5 acres) which is always above even the highest tides. The flora is restricted to salt-resistant plants with occasional wild carrot and other umbellifers. It is important mainly for its cormorant (*Phalacrocorax carbo*), colony which has been known since 1906. The 300 or so nests occupy the western side of the island and there is plenty of room for further expansion. It is probably the largest cormorant colony in the west of Ireland, and as such, deserves special protection.

Fanore Dunes

Though their total area is in excess of 60 hectares (150 acres), about half of their area is occupied by a holiday caravan encampment. The dunes themselves occupy the western fringe and give way to an area of open dune grassland on the landward side. The redistribution of sand has resulted in the exposure of limestone pavement and glacially deposited boulders.

The plant community in the dunes is dominated by marram grass (*Ammophila arenaria*) and sea bindweed (*Calystegia soldanella*). On the seaward side sea holly (*Eryngium maritimum*) is prolific in places. Some delightful flowers, like scarlet pimpernel (*Anagallis arvensis*), the sandhill pansy (*Viola tricolor curtisii*) and a variety of orchids grow in these dunes in the summer months.

In the dune hollows and behind them in the close-cropped sward are carpets of yellow bird's foot trefoil (*Lotus corniculatus*), lady's bedstraw

The sand dune system at Fanore.

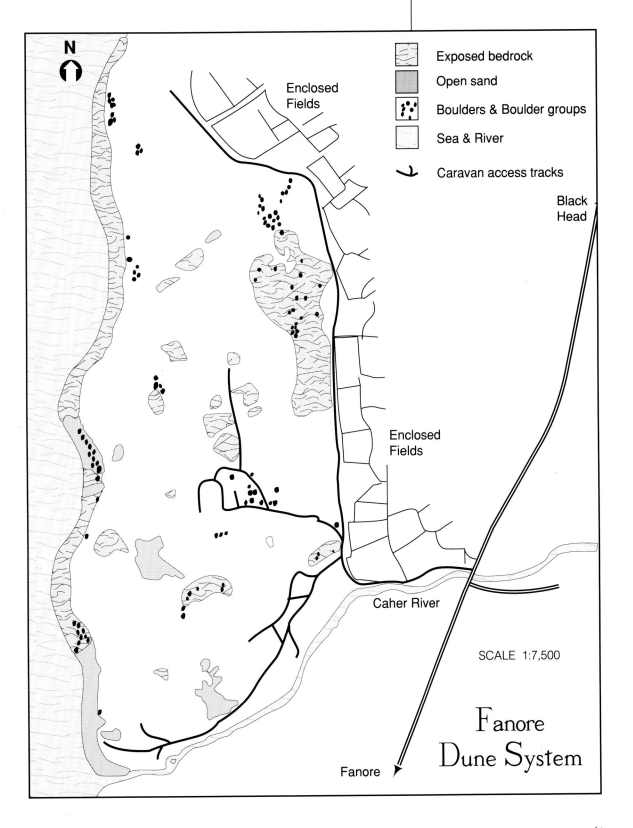

N

Exposed bedrock

Open sand

Boulders & Boulder groups

Sea & River

Caravan access tracks

Enclosed
Fields

Black
Head

Enclosed
Fields

Caher River

SCALE 1:7,500

Fanore
Dune System

Fanore

(*Galium verum*), eyebright (*Euphrasia* spp.), and at least 9 varieties of dandelion (some rare). Specialities include the creeping, red-stemmed dodder (*Cuscuta epithymum*) and in autumn the spirally twisted lady's tresses orchid (*Spiranthes spiralis*). The elusive bee orchid (*Ophrys apifera*) is also found. Among the insects the most showy are the burnet moths (Zygaenidae) and a number of butterfly species including the common blue (*Polyommatus icarus*) and the small heath (*Coenonympha pamphilus*).

The dunes support many breeding birds such as meadow pipits and skylarks and a few wheatears and stonechats (*Saxicola torquata*). A few pairs of sand martins (*Riparia r.*) nest regularly, as do one or two pairs of ringed plover (*Charadrius hiaticula*). Up to a dozen choughs (*Pyrrhocorax p.*) can be seen foraging for invertebrates in the dune turf throughout the winter.

The Rine peninsula and saltmarsh

The salt marsh is of regional importance. It is dominated by sea pink and meadow grasses but has in association sea plantain (*Plantago maritima*), sea spurrey (*Spergularia* spp.) sea aster (*Aster tripolium*) and a number of other salt-resistant plants. Sea mugwort (*Artemisia vulgaris*) is local and sea purslane (*Halimione portulacoides*) is a rarity. In the drier parts of the saltmarsh grow abundant scurvy grass and salt tolerant rushes and sedges. The dry grassland is dominated by red fescue (*Festuca rubra*) but has a variety of flowers too including storksbill (*Erodium cicutarium*) and sea sandwort (*Honkenya peploides*). The area is grazed by cattle and by rabbits (*Oryctolagus cuniculus*). Otters are common at the Rine; there are holts at a number of places along the spit.

The saltmarsh is most important for birds. In winter up to 100 each of Brent geese (*Branta bernicla*), shelduck (*Tadorna t.*) and red-breasted mergansers (*Mergus serrator*) feed there. A variety of wading birds including curlews (*Numenius arquata*) oystercatchers (*Haematopus ostralegus*) and bar-tailed godwits (*Limosa lapponica*) accompany the feeding wildfowl in winter. Good numbers of wintering wildfowl and waders can be seen in Bell Harbour too. Up to 50 shelduck and 100 teal are regular feeders there. Wading birds include redshank (*Tringa totanus*), greenshank (*Tringa nebularia*), dunlin (*Calidris alpina*), ringed plover (*Charadrius hiaticula*) and lapwing (*Vanellus v.*) but numbers tend to be small.

Lough Murree and Flaggy shore

The 14 hectare (35 acre) lake is brackish due to its subterranean connection with the sea. The flora comprises a variety of pondweeds (*Potamogeton* spp.) water mint (*Mentha aquatica*) and watercress (*Nasturtium* spp.) along the edge. Salt-tolerant plants such as buckshorn plantain (*Plantago coronopus*) and sea pearlwort (*Sagina maritima*) are found along the seaward side.

Lough Murree is thought to have one of the richest invertebrate faunas of all the Burren lakes, due partly to its position but perhaps also to nutrient enrichment from adjacent fertilised land.

In winter a variety of wildfowl are found on the lake including pochard, tufted duck, wigeon, little grebes, coots and moorhens. Up to 100 mute swans occur also and occasional whooper swans visit. A few pairs of moorhens, mute swans and little grebes nest along the margins.

The flaggy shore, including the extensive limestone reef of Carrickadda, has the abundant marine life found elsewhere along the Burren shoreline and a good deal more. Brown, green, red and coralline algae proliferate on the reef. A diverse lichen flora is evident along the Flaggy shore. More than 70 species of the three representative types are found there including many which grow only on the granite boulders.

The molluscan fauna of the reef is particularly rich with all common species represented. Sea 'hares' (*Aplysia*) are common and visible at low tide. A rare land snail species with affinities to the periwinkles was discovered at the Flaggy shore. Shellfish are regularly collected for local consumption and a regular flock of wintering oystercatchers exploit them as well.

The North Atlantic Drift washes the Burren coastline and is an important factor in the richness and diversity of its marine life. Species with southern affinities like the seaweed *Bifurcaria bifurcata* and the sea urchin *Paracentrotus lividus* are examples of this influence. The occurence of sea beans such as horse-eye and sea heart on the beach at Fanore and the occasional strandings of marine turtles of tropical origin illustrate the fact that the Burren coastline has even more distant influences.

The Rine Peninsula and saltmarsh as seen from the air.

Flora

From Algae to Angiosperms

Most of the people who visit the Burren in the summer come to admire its unique flora. People with all levels of expertise, from the casual tourist to the dedicated botanist, converge on the region to experience one of the truly remarkable natural sights to be found in western Europe. Brightly coloured wild flowers-inhabitants of a wide range of habitats, altitudes and even countries-intermingle on the fissured limestone to puzzle and delight. This chapter is by way of an explanation of this fascinating flora. It is not intended as a botanical treatise but rather as an introduction to the world of the botanist, to enable the bewildered to gain a fuller appreciation and enjoyment.

Flora means flowers but it implies more. The term includes a wide range of plants from the sophisticated orchids to the more primitive pines. However, the plant kingdom does not end here. Below the flowering plants (angiosperms) and conifers (gymnosperms) are the ferns, horsetails and clubmosses (pteridophytes); the mosses and liverworts (bryophytes); the lichens; the fungi; and lowliest of all the algae.

While it is certainly not the purpose of the book to burden the reader with taxonomic classification, nor to ponder inordinately on the inconspicuous it is nevertheless important to have some notion of the entire range of the Burren's plants and to know something of their distribution in the region. An introduction to the latter is included in Chapter 2. By visiting the various habitats outlined furnished with a good field guide the would-be botanist can expect to become familiar with a good deal more than just the gentians and the cranesbills.

A proliferation of spring gentians and early purple orchids.

Algae

Algae are thought to be one of the earliest forms of all life. Their fossil remains have been identified in the most ancient sedimentary rocks, thousands of millions of years old. The fossil remains of ancient algae (phytoplankton) which lived on or near the surface of the sea 300 million years ago form a substantial microscopic constituent of the Carboniferous limestone. Zooplankton fed on the algae and together they provided the food base for higher animals – crinoids, corals, lampshells and other creatures whose fossils are now the irregularities in the otherwise smooth grey rock.

Today, marine algae similar to those found in ancient tropical seas occur as blooms in warm summer conditions. A well publicised variety, the notorious 'red tide' is simply a red-coloured algal bloom which develops from time to time in warm summers. It has the capacity to secrete chemicals which though harmless to shellfish like oysters are toxic to those who eat them. Blooms of algae similar to the 'red tide' have been noted occasionally in Galway Bay particularly in the period 1980-2.

Algae are much more familiar along the Burren coastline in the form of seaweeds. Six or more species of brown wracks (*Fucus*) occupy the intertidal zone, from the channel wrack on the upper shore to the serrated wrack on the lower. Below them again and exposed usually only during spring tides are the yellow-brown kelps. An entire range of seaweeds from the green enteromorpha and sea lettuce (*Ulva*) to the red carragheen (*Chondrus*) and dulse or dillisk (*Palmaria*) are found at varying levels of exposure to fluctuating tides. In the rock pools, exposed by low tides along the Burren's coastline, the calcareous red algae (*Lithophyllum*) are common. Beds of detached coralline red algae known as maerl are found in shallower water near Finavarra. Though known locally as 'coral' they are, in fact, quite different, be-

Nostoc algae occupying a solution hollow in the limestone.

'Paper algae' (*Oedogonium*) draped around the turlough's swallow holes.

ing derived from plants not animals. A great display of marine algae is to be found on Carrickadda, at the Flaggy shore. Here the strange cups and straps of sea thong (*Himanthalia elongata*) abound amid the red, green, brown and coralline algae.

Algae are also found in freshwater but of the hundreds of species known from Irish freshwaters only a dozen or so are recorded from the Burren proper. Some of these, however, are notable and important. *Nostoc* is a primitive blue-green algae which acts as an erosional agent on the limestone in secreting a weak acid which steadily dissolves the rock so that the characteristic solution cups (giants' footprints) are eventually formed. These in turn form miniature gathering basins where soil and other organic debris can accumulate, providing beds on which other plants can become established.

Algal 'paper' or algal 'felt' is a strange fabric-like material often found covering the beds of dried-up turloughs. It is one of a group of surface-dwelling algae (*Oedogonium et al.*) which are greenish-brown when active but dry out in sunlight to a whitish blanket draped over rocks and around swallow holes. It is more noticeable in dry, sunny summers.

The stoneworts (*Chara* and *Nitella*) grow abundantly in the beds of more permanent water bodies where they provide food for birds like diving ducks. The status of these plants has long been the subject of dispute but they are now generally included among the algae. They form extensive white mats along the sides of those wetlands with fluctuating water tables.

A rare alga (*Cladophora sauteri*) which forms peculiar spherical balls in the water is found in Ballycullinan lake beyond the south-eastern edge of the Burren.

One other alga worthy of mention, despite the fact that its presence is only likely to be recorded by experts, is the microscopic species *Phycopeltis*. As a subaerial rather than an aquatic species it may occur in a wide range of habitats, being largely windborn. Its claim to fame is that as a species associated with the tropics it is unknown throughout most of Europe. It is found quite commonly in parts of Clare and Galway, including the Burren. As with so many Burren anomalies we are left to wonder why.

Fungi

These plants, lacking in the green pigment chlorophyll, must derive their nutrients by means other than the direct influence of sunlight. They do this either as parasites (living off other living plants) or as saprophytes (living off dead plants). They exist in a wide variety of forms, from microscopic smuts, rusts, moulds and mildews to the more familiar mushrooms and toadstools. Because of their preference for damper situations they are not particularly well represented in the Burren, though certain habitats (beneath hazel scrub) have a good variety of recognisable forms. They have apparently never been thoroughly studied by a mycologist (fungi specialist) so perhaps there are interesting discoveries to come.

Well known edible species like field and horse mushrooms (*Agaricus* spp.), ink cap (*Coprinus*); parasol (*Lepiota*) and champignon (*Clitocybe*) are common and widespread in reclaimed fields and pasture around the Burren (as elsewhere in the country). The prime growing (and collecting) time is in autumn. In undisturbed, unfertilised Burren grassland fungi are scarcer but unusual varieties may be found in autumn and into early winter. Puffballs (*Lycoperdon*) or earth balls are widespread though they are often overlooked unless accidentally kicked, when they release their cloud of brown spore dust into the air. Milk fungi (*Lactarius*) though local, may occur almost anywhere in the Burren and are even found in the coarse grassland of the high plateau. They are identified by their overall creamy colour and their prominent veining at the top of the stipe (stalk) and in the depression on the cap which deepens with age. The penny bun fungus (*Boletus*) has been found growing on the side of Mullaghmore, entirely in the open. Both milk cap and boletus are ground storey plants associated with hardwoods, so it is interesting to find them growing in the open Burren. Their presence would suggest the previous existence of deciduous woodland at high levels.

Agarics sprouting from a cowpat.

The dunes at Fanore have a well-developed fungus community. In the dune hollows, in association with dwarf willow, may be found dull-coloured species of the genus *Inocybe*. Puffballs are common amid the short-cropped dune grasses. Here too can be found small, colourful fungi like the dune agarics. The red-capped, yellow-stemmed *Hygrocybe* occurs in little groups in September and *Stropharia*, with their orange-yellow caps are found both in the dunes and elsewhere in pasture.

The greatest variety of fungi is found in the Burren's scrub, in the mature deciduous woodlands like Garryland and in the spruce and pine plantations in and around the region. Species like wood agaric (*Collybia*), honey fungi (*Armillariella*) and Velvet shank (*Flammulina*) can be found growing throughout the winter. Bracket fungi (*Coriolus, Ganoderma*) are common on the rotting trunks of trees and a variety of saprophytes including the toxic brown roll-rim (*Paxillus involutus*) are found in the decaying leaf litter of the woodland floor.

Some fungi are highly specific in their choice of habitat. The Jew's ear (*Auricularia auricula-judae*) for example, is found primarily on the branches of elder and is easily recognised by its pink fleshy cups which indeed bear a vague resemblance to a human ear. Cowpats often provide little nutrient-rich oases on which fungi can grow. Agarics are commonly found growing in these situations.

Lichens

A lichen is a sandwich of an alga and a fungus. The alga is the 'meat' in the sandwich which sustains the fungus while being protected from desiccation by the latter's outer layer. Lichens are thus able to withstand long periods of drought and can survive and colonise situations prohibitive to other types of plants.

Lichens can be subdivided into three groups: crustose (flat, featureless, looking like stains on rocks); foliose (looking leafy-edged); and fruticose (looking like ragged tufts). All three types are well represented in the Burren, the crustose-type dominating on the open rock while the others are commonest in the scrub and other woodland.

Of some 350 species occurring in the Burren the known Irish distribution of about 17 is confined to the region and the Aran Islands. Two found as recently as 1984 were not previously known from Ireland or Britain and one found near the outfall of the Caher river near Fanore, *Arthopyrenia caesia*, was not known elsewhere outside continental Europe.

Though crustose lichens are widespread on the open pavement, the best concentrations are on the stone walls and boulders with which the region is liberally endowed. A small number are very common with *Collema* (blackish), *Aspicilia* (whitish) and *Caloplaca* (orange) predominating. Boulders that are regular bird perches are gifted with nutrient enrichment and support an abundant, diverse lichen flora. Silicon rather than calcium is a major constituent of the granite erratics. Their lichens are therefore silicolous rather than calcicolous. A prolific growth of silicolous crustose lichens including *Rhizocarpon richardii* and *Lecanora* spp. occur on these granite boulders, particularly along the coast near Finavarra.

Discrete lichen zonation, typical of rocky shores generally is common at Finavarra and elsewhere along the Burren coastline. Here the succession from the black tar lichen (*Verrucaria*) in the littoral zone, to the yellow/orange *Caloplaca* and *Xanthoria* of the splash zone, with the blackish *Lichina confinis* and the brown *Pyrenocollema halodytes*, is clearly evident. Many more species of *Verrucaria* are found on the open limestone.

In the sand dunes at Fanore a very different lichen flora is found in the transition zone between the marram grasses and the close-cropped sward. It comprises a number of foliose types including *Collema tenax* and *Squamarina cartilaginea*.

The richest habitat for lichens is in the scrubby woodland where the damp humid conditions

Crustose and foliose lichens in shore splash zone.

Above: *Xanthoria parietina* on shoreline limestone.
Below: *Parmeliella plumbea* on hazel.

are conducive to their growth. On the bark, branches and twigs of hazel, ash, blackthorn and whitethorn, and to a lesser degree a few others, all three types of lichen are found in rich abundance. The hazel branches may be festooned with a succession of species. These range from *Tomasellia gelatinosa* on the twigs to intermediates like *Arthonia tumidula* and the final colonisers, the greyish foliose lichens *Parmeliella plumbea* and *Pannaria rubiginosa*. Where the scrub is dense a variety of other lichens occur on the bark and branches which include the beautiful *Graphis* species. In particularly closed impenetrable places mosses and liverworts take the place of the lichen flora.

The branches and twigs of thorn bushes support a diverse lichen flora comprising tufts of *Ramalina*, *Usnea* and *Evernia prunastri*. Crustose species include *Lecanora chlarotera* and *Lecanora carpinea*.

In the mossy ground cover beneath the hazel scrub occasional dog lichen (*Peltigera*) can be found. Occurring here and there is *P. praetextata*, chocolate brown with distinctive filamentous white undersides.

On the shale outliers in the western Burren the acid heath supports abundant deer moss (in fact a fruticose lichen, *Cladonia rangiformis*) with *Cladina arbuscula* and *Cladina portentosa*. The wax-red fruiting caps of *Cladonia coccifera* combined with the ragged plant itself are highly photogenic, as are many of the Burren's lichens.

Due to the fact that lichens absorb water and gases directly from the air (not having a root system) they are in most cases sensitive to atmospheric pollution. In locations where aerial pollution is concentrated most lichens gradually disappear. Only a few like *Lecanora conizaeoides*, an industrial lichen not found in the Burren, can withstand the effects of pollutant gases like sulphur dioxide. Lichens grow very slowly (a millimetre or two per year) but are generally very long-lived. Pollution has the effect of retarding this very slow but steady outward growth.

The construction of the Moneypoint power station on the south Clare coast, with its attendant sulphur dioxide (and other) gaseous emissions, has prompted a monitoring programme in the Burren since 1986. A number of pollution-sensitive herbs, mosses and particularly lichens have been monitored in various sites, mainly in the eastern Burren to try to gauge the detrimental effect (if any) on the Burren flora.

Parmelia perlata on blackthorn (right).

Ramalina siliquosa above (on granite erratic) and right.

Above: Peltigera canina (dog lichen).
Right: Cladonia fimbriata.

Above: fruticose and foliose lichens festooning a blackthorn.
Below: Opegrapha sp. on birch.

Lichens

BOX 4

Biomonitoring air quality in the Burren

The quality of the air in the Burren has been monitored annually by scientists since 1986 (the year of opening of the Moneypoint Power station in south Clare).

Most of the monitoring is being carried out in the eastern Burren at some 26 - 28 sites. Lichens and bryophytes are the primary subjects of the monitoring programme. A number of known sensitive plants including bracken (*Pteridium aquilinum*) and flora such as wild violet (*Viola riviniana*), the blackberry family (*Rubus* spp.), nettle (*Urtica dioica*), some ten tree species and a number of herbaceous species are also monitored. The lichens being monitored are divided into groups depending on their degree of sensitivity to pollution:

Moderately sensitive: *Lobaria pulmonaria,*
Collema furfuraceum,
Parmelia perlata and
Parmelia caperata.

Sensitive: *Usnea fragilescens,*
Nephroma laevigatum,
Pannaria rubiginosa,
Parmeliella plumbea and
Sticta spp.

Highly Sensitive: *Sticta sylvatica.*

Moderately sensitive mosses: *Homalothecium sericeum* and
Orthotrichum anomalum.

Mosses and Liverworts

Mosses and liverworts are grouped together as bryophytes and are regarded as primitive green plants having no true vascular system but subsisting by absorbing rainfall directly. Mosses are usually characterised by their tightly packed water-saturated structures. The damp-loving liverworts exist in two distinct forms; a lobed type and a leafy type.

In the open, dry conditions of the Burren these plants are sparse, despite the relatively abundant bryophyte flora of the normally wet west of Ireland. Cushions of *Tortella* and *Breutelia* moss are common in places where moisture is retained. These moss cushions may be of enormous size, sometimes totally occupying a substantial fissure in the limestone. In shaded, damp situations out of the drying effects of wind and sun the distinctively glossy, flattened moss *Neckera crispa* is in evidence. In these

The upper flood limit of a turlough is clearly recorded by the blackish moss *Cinclidotus fontinaloides*.

circumstances there are also a number of leafy liverworts. The very dark green *Marchesinia mackaii* grows in considerable profusion in places, along with other yellowish-green varieties. In the small north-facing caves and wet overhangs near Black Head a number of these bryophytes may be found together. Six species of mosses unknown elsewhere in County Clare have been identified in the dunes at Fanore.

The hazel scrub of the Burren, with its high humidity and damp ground-cover is full of bryophytes. Often they grow in such abundance that they completely carpet the woodland floor to such a depth as to preclude other ground-storey plants. In circumstances where the ground is rock-strewn mosses will grow on top of the wet boulders, a metre or more from the actual ground level. One of the commonest mosses is *Hylocomium splendens* which, as the Latin name suggests, is a splendid glossy yellow-brown moss on reddish stems. It is accompanied by a number of other common mosses including *Ctenidium molluscum* and *Hypnum cupressiforme*, which actually grows around the saturated bases of the trees themselves. In places these mosses support a lichen flora which includes the strange *Peltigera* with its filamentous underside and leathery grey upperside.

The Burren's wetlands have characteristic mosses too, like the showy *Drepanocladus* spp. which are found on the sides of the fenny lakes near Mullaghmore. At Lough Bunny, which always retains water but has a fluctuating water level, grows *Bryum neodamense*, a very rare reddish-green moss, and not far from the lake, in turlough conditions, is found *Calliergon trifarium* in its only Irish station.

The turloughs have clearly zoned mosses which are revealed in dry circumstances in the summer. Growing as a distinct band at the level of normal winter flooding is the blackish moss *Cinclidotus fontinaloides*. This is a character species for turloughs and even in high summer the moss can be seen bedecking rocks, posts, and even those branches of thorn bushes which are normally inundated in winter. At lower than flood level and often covering much of the turlough floor is the more robust-looking green moss *Fontinalis antipyretica*. This aquatic moss is less capable of withstanding long-term drying and desiccation.

Ferns, clubmosses and horsetails

These are vascular plants and are grouped together botanically under the heading pteridophytes. They are a very ancient group, their fossil remains having been identified in Old Red Sandstone layers in County Kilkenny, dating from around 400 million years ago. Indeed, gigantic ferns, clubmosses and horsetails were in their heyday in the terrestrial phase of the Carboniferous which, before it was removed by Ice Age glaciers, once covered the Burren.

In ancient times pteridophytes were able to proliferate because of lack of competition; nowadays they form a mere fraction of the Irish flora, with some 50 species, about 35 of which occur in the Burren.

There can be little doubt that, before Victorian times ferns were more abundant than they are now. They were widely collected in the Burren (and elsewhere) in that period. The much reduced royal fern (*Osmunda regalis*) which is still found in the east Burren wetlands was once avidly collected for ornamentation.

There are about 25 fern species in the Burren, almost two-thirds of the total for Ireland. Many, like the lime-loving rustyback, (*Ceterach officinarum*), the hart's tongue (*Phyllitis scolopendrium*) and the tiny wall rue (*Asplenium ruta-muraria*) are ubiquitous, and even the normally lime-shunning bracken (*Pteridium aquilinum*) has managed to establish itself, particularly in reclaimed and abandoned fields.

Top: rustyback fern with wall rue and maidenhair spleenworts.
Centre: gold on silver – an autumnal bracken frond against limestone.
Bottom: Hart's tongue fern.

Two strange-looking small ferns, the adder's tongue (*Ophioglossum vulgatum*) and the moonwort (*Botrychium lunaria*) are found in the Burren. They do not survive land reclamation and, particularly in the case of the moonwort, are fickle in their appearances. Both occur in grassland – the former often favouring turlough country.

Spleenworts are represented by a few species, notably the widespread maidenhair spleenwort (*Asplenium trichomanes*), the black spleenwort (*Asplenium adiantum-nigrum*), which is more local, and the sea spleenwort (*Asplenium marinum*) which is commonest along the Burren's west-facing coastline.

All three Irish species of polypody fern (*australe*, *interjectum* and *vulgare*) are found in the Burren. Though difficult to distinguish in the field *Polypodium australe* is found mainly in limestone grikes, in preference to the saddles in tree trunks favoured by *Polypodium vulgare*. The shield-ferns (*Polystichum*), buckler ferns (*Dryopteris*) and brittle-bladder fern (*Cystopteris fragilis*) are all well represented in the region.

The Burren has its specialities too. The delicate marsh fern (*Thelypteris palustris*) once widely collected, still survives in a few marshy places in the eastern sector. The Wilson's filmy fern (*Hymenophyllum wilsonii*) though found in a number of places throughout Ireland is restricted to one locality in the Burren. But pride of place must go to the beautiful maidenhair fern (*Adiantum capillus-veneris*) which, as one of Ireland's few representatives of the Mediterranean flora, is more or less restricted to the Burren. Though much reduced by collecting it is still found in a number of localities throughout the region.

Clubmosses are not well represented in the Burren. Only two of the five Irish species occur. The lesser clubmoss (*Selaginella selaginoides*) is found particularly in the eastern wetlands while *Huperzia selago* (generally an upland species) occurs on one or two of the Burren's mountains.

In contrast, the Burren's wetlands are good places for horsetails, with six species and at least two hybrids known to occur. While the common horsetail (*Equisetum arvense*), the water horsetail (*Equisetum fluviatile*) and the marsh horsetail (*Equisetum palustre*) are widespread, the wood horsetail (*Equisetum sylvaticum*), the variegated horsetail (*Equisetum variegatum*) and the largest, the great horsetail (*Equisetum telmateia*) are decidedly local or rare.

The mare's tail (*Hippuris vulgaris*) is often incorrectly identified as a horsetail: it has a similar feathery structure of whorled 'branches'. Despite this superficial resemblance, it is unrelated, being a higher, flowering plant.

The higher plants

Higher plants are divided into two main groups, the conifers (gymnosperms) and all others (angiosperms). They are represented in the Burren by some 650 species-about two thirds of the total found in the whole of Ireland.

Conifers

There are only three native Irish conifers: the scots pine (*Pinus sylvestris*), the yew (*Taxus baccata*) and the juniper (*Juniperus communis*). All three are found in the Burren though the first, considered to have become extinct in historicial times, has been reintroduced in modern times. Scots pine was widely planted with the establishment of the demesnes at the end of the seventeenth and the beginning of the eighteenth centuries. Though also planted on a widespread basis in state plantations it is less commerically viable than introduced nearctic species like lodgepole pine (*Pinus contorta*).

The yew was also common and widespread in limestone districts. It has been extensively removed by man due to its toxicity to livestock (which does not prevent it from being lightly grazed by goats). Isolated straggly yews still manage to survive on rocky escarpments throughout the region and in one or two places (e.g. near Lough Muckanagh) there are pockets of stunted yew trees on the limestone pavement. In Garryland wood there is a pocket of about 100 fine yew trees which have been unaffected by grazing.

Juniper is found throughout the region growing as a spiky-leaved prostrate shrub (the yew is distinctly soft-leaved to the touch). In many localities it is an abundant feature and on the uplands may be a major component of the heathland community. In the turlough country west of Gort it grows extensively on rocky outcrops and islands. Being so spiky it is little grazed. Juniper produces berry-like cones in the autumn which are at first green then bluish-black, quite different from the red berry-cones of the yew.

Shrubs and deciduous trees

The limestone supports an extremely abundant shrub flora which, if grazing were withdrawn would undoubtedly invade most of the region, overshadowing the grasses and other herbs in the competition for sunlight and nutrients. In places where grazing is restricted, scrub, notably hazel (*Corylus avellana*), whitethorn (*Crataegus monogyna*) and blackthorn (*Prunus spinosa*) invade relentlessly and would eventually become an understorey to a climax cover of trees like ash (*Fraxinus excelsior*). The hazel has been cut back so frequently that it is multi-stemmed or coppiced throughout. Holly (*Ilex aquifolium*) is also an abundant understorey plant growing occasionally in little copses. Buckthorn or purging buckthorn (*Rhamnus catharticus*), which may be easily distinguished by it asymmetrical leaf veining is less common than other thorns: alder buckthorn (*Frangula alnus*) is decidedly scarce, occurring mainly

Blackthorn fruits (sloes).

in prostrate form near a few of the turloughs. Whitebeam (*Sorbus aria*) and rowan or mountain ash (*Sorbus aucuparia*) appear to be local but when berry-laden in autumn can be found in ones and twos throughout the open country and in hedgerows. Spindle trees (*Euonymus europaeus*), guelder roses (*Viburnum opulus*) and elders (*Sambucus nigra*) are widespread in hedges and along roadsides. They may occur also in prostrate from in the limestone pavement. Other fruiting trees like wild damson (*Prunus domestica*) and crab apple (*Malus sylvestris*) are scarce.

Ivy (*Hedera helix*) and honeysuckle (*Lonicera periclymenum*) are characteristic creeping shrubs of the grikes in the open limestone. Dogwood (*Cornus sanguinea*) occurs occasionally in the grikes and in hedges but is apparently on the decline. Gorse or furze (*Ulex europaeus*), which favours acid soils is scarce in the region though it grows in pockets along the eastern and southern boundary.

Of the potential deciduous tree cover, ash is easily most significant. Oak (*Quercus robur* and *Q. petraea*) were once widespread in the valleys and on western slopes but have long since been felled. The nearest sizeable stands of oak are to be found at Dromore (near Ennis) and at Garryland (near Gort). Elm (*Ulmus glabra*) was probably once widespread on the slopes and valleys of the Burren but can now only be found scattered in the hedges (where they have managed to avoid Dutch elm disease). A little elm wood, thought to be native, exists beside Mullaghmore, a fragment perhaps of what much of the Burren slopes once looked like.

Spindle in autumnal splendour.

BOX 5

Naturalised flowers of the Burren

Not all the Burren flowers are truly wild. At least 10 per cent of the plants are escapees from gardens or plants that have become naturalised as a result of conscious or unconscious importation by man. An example is the fairy foxglove (*Erinus alpinus*) which grows on the famous pinnacle well on the roadside between Ballyvaughan and Black Head. On the hillside adjacent to the well it is accompanied by another non-native, columbine (*Aquilegia vulgaris*).

On the north side of Abbey Hill grows red valerian (*Centranthus ruber*) in naturalised profusion and it occurs in other places where it has escaped from gardens.

Other notable examples are traveller's joy (*Clematis vitalba*) and the white stonecrop (*Sedum album*). Cotoneaster (*Cotoneaster microphyllus*), and snowberry (*Symphoricarpos albus*) are common garden shrubs often planted in hedges. Both appear to have become naturalised in a few Burren localities.

Alder (*Alnus glutinosa*) and downy birch (*Betula pubescens*) are understandably scarce; conditions favour neither species. In a few localities, like the Caher valley, aspen (*Populus tremula*) can be found.

Beech (*Fagus sylvatica*) was first introduced into demesnes in the seventeenth century. It is now widespread along roadsides and in the woodlands of the Burren's valleys. Beech and other species have been planted by the Department of Forestry (Coillte) alongside plantations in an effort to ease the visual impact of the unattractive dark blocks of conifers.

Ten of the 14 Irish species of willow are found in the Burren though some of these are undoubtedly naturalised (not from native stock). The creeping willow (*Salix repens*) is widespread on the hills and in the limestone pavement where it hugs the ground as a low shrub. It is also found in the dune hollows at Fanore.

Bog myrtle (*Myrica gale*), though absent from the limestone proper, grows in abundance along the shores of many of the lakes and other boggy wetlands. Evidence of its having occupied Burren wetlands since the last Ice Age exists in the accumulated sediments in the beds of some of the peripheral lakes.

Many different varieties of the blackberry (*Rubus fruticosis*) have been identified in the region. They are probably commonest (and most accessible for their rich harvest) along the network of stone walls. In the open limestone the blackberry is largely replaced by the stone bramble (*Rubus saxatilis*) which favours a prostrate, creeping form. Dewberry (*Rubus caesius*) fruits look like blackberries, though with few composite segments. This plant is

Frosted fruit: blackberries.

more local than the others, showing a preference for the edges of turloughs. Wild raspberry (*Rubus idaeus*) is found in certain localities like the Glen of Clab. With wild strawberry (*Fragaria vesca*) it provides tasty refreshment to scrubland ramblers.

Three species of rose flourish in the Burren. The most widespread and the 'character species' of most of the eastern and central Burren is the burnet rose (*Rosa pimpinellifolia*), which grows everywhere amid the shattered limestone. Its crimson fruits or hips add distinctive colour to its habitat. The dog rose (*Rosa canina*) and the downy rose (*Rosa sherardii*) are widespread but tend to be restricted to the hedges.

The heath community which is found mainly on the northern-facing Burren hills is comprised mainly of ling (*Calluna vulgaris*) with two heaths (*Erica* spp.). Occasional bilberry (*Vaccinium myrtillus*) is also found but the most interesting berry-bearers are crowberry (*Empetrum nigrum*) and bearberry (*Arctostaphylos uva-ursi*) which are montane species associated normally with much colder places than the Burren.

BOX 6

The Burren Climate

The climate of the west of Ireland is described generally as Atlantic, being influenced to a major extent by oceanic conditions. The air flow is predominantly from the south-west and west, of mean annual windspeed F 2.5-5 on the Beaufort scale. Gales are relatively frequent particularly during the winter months.

High levels of precipitation are characteristic of the west coast with up to 2,800 millimetres (110 inches) of annual rainfall in parts of Connemara. Mean annual rainfall in the Burren ranges from about 1,000 millimetres (39 inches) to 1,400 millimetres (55 inches) which is, in general, low for the west of Ireland.

Annual sunshine ranges from 1300 to 1400 hours which is about average for most of the midlands and the south-west of the country. High levels of evapotranspiration (evaporation of moisture from plants) are characteristic of the Burren with relatively high average values in summer 425 millimetres (16.5 inches) and in winter 125 millimetres (5 inches).

The mean daily air temperature is high both in summer and the winter: 5.5-6.5°C in January; 15°C in July. Frosts are consequently infrequent and are generally confined to the period 15 November-15 April (over the period 1944-1968). The grass growing season is long, averaging from 1 March to 15 December.

Investigation of the temperature gradients near the surface of the limestone rock has shown that on warm sunny days the rock surface may be 8°C higher than the adjacent air. In contrast the air temperature within the grikes may be 10°C lower than air temperature. The heat storage capacity of the limestone combined with the temperature gradients near its surface have an important bearing on the distribution of the flora.

Flowers

There is no single reason why the Burren holds such amazingly abundant and varied flowers. Factors such as climate, geographic location and altitude have a bearing, but the limestone and the thin veneer of rich overlying soils (where these exist) are of primary importance.

The limestone has physical characteristics conducive to growth, such as its capacity to absorb

The species-rich limestone grassland of the Burren.

heat, to provide sheltered pockets in its crevices and hollows and to break down easily into a crumbled surface, thus permitting easy rooting. But there are important chemical and biological factors too.

The limestone soils (rendzinas) vigorously promote the growth of micro-organisms (bacteria) which make that most important nutrient nitrate, available. They do this by synthesising it from the air (which is mostly nitrogen). The process is called nitrogen fixing. The limestone contains the other nutrients necessary for growth but only in small quantity. Consequently plant growth is encouraged but at a measured rate. Early invading herbs do not grow so vigorously as to smother out the grasses and other plants and so Burren meadowland is marvellously rich. There may be 40 or 50 species in an area as small as 4 square metres (4.8 sq yards). A dozen or more of these species may be grasses.

Two main grassland types occupy the Burren. That of the majority of the region grows on the thin rendzina soils (where these occur) and is typified by a particular assemblage of grasses

Managed pasture on the thicker soils: species-poor compared to the limestone grasslands.

and other herbs. Flowers such as various orchids, rough hawkbit (*Leontodon hispidus*), carline thistle (*Carlina vulgaris*), kidney vetch (*Anthyllis vulneraria*), yellow-wort (*Blackstonia perfoliata*), Salad burnet (*Sanguisorba minor*), and autumn gentian (*Gentianella amarella*) are all typical of this kind of grassland. Typical grasses are the lovely blue moor-grass (*Sesleria albicans*) and the even more attractive quaking grass (*Briza media*). (Botanists have defined this kind of grassland by a particular plant association: mountain avens and slender St John's wort, which typify it in the Burren).

On thicker deposits (as in the north-eastern valleys) the assemblage *Centaureo-Cynosuretum*, so called because of the typical association of purple knapweeds and dog's tail grass, replaces the normal limestone grassland. The plants here are more commonplace agricultural species and include fescues (*Festuca rubra*) and clovers (*Trifolium* spp.). Among the flowers which distinguish this type of grassland are the cowslip (*Primula veris*), lady's bedstraw (*Galium verum*), burnet saxifrage (*Pimpinella saxifraga*), wild carrot (*Daucus carota*) and bulbous buttercup (*Ranunculus bulbosus*).

Of course, depending on factors such as proximity to the sea, altitude and recent man-modification (including the use of fertilisers and herbicides) the boundaries of these categories may become obscured. Nevertheless they constitute the botanical framework into which the greater part of the flora of the limestone land fits.

Most people who go to the Burren for the first time are overawed by the sheer complexity of the numbers of plant species and assemblages and their significance in a regional, national or international context. A simple guide of 'noteworthy' plants which may help reduce the hundreds of species to a manageable significant fraction is as follows (Webb, 1961). The grasses: heath grass (*Danthonia decumbens*), sheep's fescue (*Festuca ovina*), false brome (*Brachypodium sylvaticum*) and fern grass (*Desmazeria rigida*) are widespread. There are, however more than 50 grasses in the Burren most of which are fairly widespread. Some noteworthy flowers are: hairy rockcress (*Arabis hirsuta*), whitlow grass (*Erophilia verna*), thale cress (*Arabidopsis thaliana*), fairy flax (*Linum catharticum*), bloody cranesbill (*Geranium sanguineum*), herb robert (*Geranium robertianum*), bird's foot trefoil (*Lotus corniculatus*), sanicle (*Sanicula europaea*), wild madder (*Rubia peregrina*), the bedstraws (*Galium* spp.), squinancywort (*Asperata odorata*), devil's bit scabious (*Succisa pratensis*), golden rod (*Solidago virgaurea*), mountain everlasting (*Antennaria dioica*), ragwort (*Senecio jacobaea*), mouse-ear hawkweed (*Hieracium pilosella*), wall lettuce (*Mycelis muralis*), prickly sow-thistle (*Sonchus asper*), harebell (*Campanula rotundifolia*), primrose (*Primula vulgaris*), eyebright (*Euphrasia* spp.), wild thyme (*Thymus* spp.) and wood sage (*Teucrium scorodonia*) which were regarded as common more or less throughout the region. Most are also fairly common elsewhere in the country (particularly on limestone) but on the Burren they are stunningly abundant.

Many other flowers are found throughout the region besides, such as the diminutive milkwort (*Polygala vulgaris*) which is normally ink-blue but varies in colour to pink, self heal (*Prunella vulgaris*), St John's wort (*Hypericum* spp.) – represented by no less than seven species in the Burren – and the delightful spring sandwort (*Minuartia verna*).

Unobtrusive tiny flowers abound. These include sticky mouse-ear (*Cerastium glomeratum*), chickweed (*Stellaria media*), lesser meadow-rue (*Thalictrum minus*), shepherd's purse

Noteworthy Burren plants.
Top: bloody cranesbill (*Geranium sanguineum*).
Centre: harebell (*Campanula rotundifolia*).
Bottom: wall lettuce (*Mycelis muralis*).

Noteworthy Burren Plants

Left: Herb-Robert (*Geranium robertianum*).

Above: Lady's bedstraw (*Galium verum*).
Left: Squinancywort (*Asperula cynanchica*).

Right: Mountain everlasting (*Antennaria dioica*).
Below: Common milkwort (*Polygala vulgaris*) and bird's foot trefoil (*Lotus corniculatus*).

Below: Wood sage (*Teucrium scorodonia*).

Left: Ox-eye daisy.
Above: Biting stonecrop.

(*Capsella bursa-pastoris*) and rue-leaved saxifrage (*Saxifraga tridactylites*) among many others.

Certain flowers are most obvious along roadsides-like the scented, pink, wild marjoram (*Origanum vulgare*) and the yellow-centred, white-headed, ox-eye daisy (*Leucanthemum vulgare*), which shake their showy heads in the draught from passing traffic. Others like the daisy (*Bellis perennis*) and the dandelion are so commonplace as to be ignored. But dandelions should not be ignored in the Burren for they are represented by at least twenty varieties, a few of which are decidedly rare.

Of course, there are noticeable changes in the flora at different times throughout the year: the flowering seasons are staggered to coincide with other vital propagation factors like the hatching of pollinating insects.

Below: Burnet rose.

Orchids

No group of flowers illustrates this process better than the orchids whose brightly coloured spike-heads illuminate the Burren grasslands throughout the summer. These sophisticated plants require a special root relationship with a fungus

Early purple orchid (*Orchis mascula*)

Bird's nest orchid (*Neottia nidus-avis*)

Dense-flowered orchid (*Neotinea maculata*)

Heath spotted-orchid (*Dactylorhiza maculata*)

Common spotted (*Dactylorhiza fuchsii* subsp: *okellyi*)

Early marsh-orchid (*Dactylorhiza incarnata*)

Western marsh-orchid (*Dactylorhiza majalis*)

Fly orchid (*Ophrys insectifera*)

Bee orchid (*Ophrys apifera*)

Lesser butterfly-orchid (*Platanthera bifolia*)

Fragrant orchid (*Gymnadenia conopsea*)

Pyramidal orchid (*Anacamptis pyramidalis*)

Twayblade (*Listera ovata*)

Frog orchid (*Coeloglossum viride*)

Autumn lady's-tresses (*Spiranthes spiralis*)

Broad-leaved helleborine (*Epipactis helleborine*)

Dark-red helleborine (*Epipactis atrorubens*)

Marsh helleborine (*Epipactis palustris*)

in order to sprout a spike of flower-heads, and consequently their appearance from year to year in the same place is somewhat unpredictable. They are pollinated by a wide range of insects from butterflies to beetles, and are in their fullest glory to coincide with the life cycle of their guests. First to appear is the early purple orchid (*Orchis mascula*) which always comes before the end of April. Their crimson spikes cover acre upon acre of the open country like a forest of miniature trees by mid-May. In late April the strange chlorophyll-lacking bird's nest orchid (*Neottia nidus-avis*) also emerges from the leaf litter in the shade of trees-but it is very local. The next to emerge is the dense-flowered orchid (*Neotinea maculata*), which thrusts up its tiny whitish flower spikes in early May. By mid-May the *Dactylorhiza* group are beginning to show. First, the marsh orchids, (*D. incarnata*) and (*D. majalis*) emerge followed by the spotted orchid (*D. fuchsii*) with its fabulous white variety *okellyi*. By the end of the month usually, the earliest fly orchids (*Ophrys insectifera*) and bee orchids (*Ophrys apifera*) are in evidence, with to their remarkable insect-like flowerheads they are more difficult to find than most other species.

June invariably 'bursts out all over' with orchids. The delicate creamy white butterfly orchid (*Platanthera bifolia*) is in evidence particularly in dampish ground. *Platanthera chlorantha*, the greater butterfly orchid, however is rare. The equally delicate (and scented) fragrant orchid (*Gymnadenia conopsea*) and the pyramidal orchid (*Anacamptis pyramidalis*) appear in the latter part of the month together with the comparatively dingy twayblade (*Listera ovata*), whose flowers look like a dozen or so tiny green men. Another small greenish species, the frog orchid (*Coeloglossum viride*) whose flower caps do indeed look like frogs' heads, emerges later than most, in early July. It is accompanied by some of the Burren's most beautiful orchids, the helleborines (*Epipactis* spp.). The rather non descript but elegant broad-leaved helleborine (*E. helleborine*) is found mainly in the more open parts of the hazel scrub while the dark red helleborine (*E. atrorubens*) favours limestone crevices, particularly at altitude. The marsh helleborine (*E. palustris*) with its most pleasing pastel colours is confined to wetter habitats.

Though many of the orchids continue to blossom throughout the summer, the latest to emerge is the tiny spiralled autumn lady's tresses (*Spiranthes spiralis*), which is unusual before the end of August. All in all there are more than 20 orchid species flowering in the Burren in an average year but some are decidedly local and have to be looked for. Due to the extent of the unfertilised grasslands and the super-abundance of insect pollinators, the majority of the Burren's orchids are commoner there than elsewhere in the country. In full flower they are certainly one of the region's spectacles.

Flowering plants of the wetlands

Just as grasses provide the backdrop against which the terrestrial flowers are set, so their wetland equivalents (reeds, sedges, rushes) provide a bland setting for a multitude of others. White or whitish flowers like grass of Parnassus (*Parnassia palustris*) and lady's smock (*Cardamine pratensis*) stand out clearly in the damp olive-coloured pasture in which they occur. The white tufts of cotton-grass (*Eriophorum*), which is really a sedge, provide striking relief to the uniform greenness of the summer wetlands.

Pink flowers are also common in summer. The straggling pink petals of the ragged robin

(*Lychnis flos-cuculi*) are abundant in the ditches and damp rushy patches, particularly on the badly drained shale. The crimson star-shaped heads of the marsh cinquefoil (*Potentilla palustris*) can be seen both in the more acid, boggy areas and in places in the calcareous fens and lake shores. A few of the marsh orchids are

Left: cotton-grass in fen vegetation.
Above: grass of Parnassus.
Below left: marsh cinquefoil.
Below: ragged robin.

Yellow iris/yellow flag.

also pink or red. Blue or bluish flowers of the wetlands tend to be small and have to be looked for. The delightful water forget-me-not (*Myosotis scorpioides*) is indeed unforgettable, easily surpassing its dryland counterpart (*M. arvensis*) in form and intensity of colour. Wild iris (*Iris pseudacorus*) decorates the fenny pasture in May and June. Its gorgeous yellow flags are held a metre or more above the damp, illuminating the wetlands in summer. There are many other yellow wetland flowers but they are invariably outshone by the splendid yellow flag.

The vegetational zonation of the turloughs is defined by a couple of yellow flowers. At the upper level of normal flooding in a number of the turloughs grows the beautiful but rare shrubby cinquefoil (*Potentilla fruticosa*) – a woody shrub which sports large yellow flowers. Below this and occupying most of the dry turlough floor is an assemblage of a few species of flood-tolerant plants, which include silverweed (*Potentilla anserina*) so named because of the silvery undersides to its leaves. In summer its bright, lemon-yellow flowers light up the otherwise lack lustre turlough floor. But they are not the only flowers in evidence: a more subtle indicator of zonation is provided by the turlough's violets. Both the wood violet (*Viola reichenbachiana*) and the dog violet (*Viola riviniana*) grow on the ground beneath the thorn-bushes which typically surround the turloughs. The dog violet, unlike its near relative will grow a few metres beyond the 'thorn line' and into the flood zone. Next is the heath dog violet (*Viola canina*). This pretty little flower has a bright yellow spur at the back, making it easy to identify. Lastly, the rare fen or turlough violet (*Viola persicifolia*), an even smaller plant with extremely delicate flowers of the palest blue, a whitish spur and spear-shaped leaves occurs (in some turloughs only) down to the lowest levels. The flowering regime of these violets coincides with the receding water level: wood and dog violets are often in flower in early April while the turlough violet is not in full flower until early June.

The major wetland system extending along the edge of the eastern Burren is partially comprised of shallow fenland in which there is a fluctuating water-table. Substantial permanent lakes exist at either end. A view from high ground (or from the air) illustrates the clearly zoned pattern of the wetland vegetation of this system. This is best viewed in late summer when the subtle colour variation and texture caused by the dominance of different wetland plants such as reeds, sedges or rushes is at its clearest. In winter much of the wetland is open water and the vegetation is a uniform ochreous colour. It is nevertheless clearly demarcated from the grey limestone and the yellow-green grassland which borders it.

This grassland is rich in species like quaking grass (*Briza media*), red fescue (*Festuca rubra*) and the purple-blue flower heads of devil's bit scabious (*Succisa pratensis*) in the autumn. Glaucous sedge (*Carex flacca*), Ox-eye daisy (*Leucanthemum vulgare*), tormentil (*Potentilla erecta*) and heath grass (*Danthonia decumbens*) are constant floral associates but 50

Heath dog-violet.

or more species are commonplace in the lakeside grassland. In areas of cut-away fen (e.g. adjacent to the Ballyeighter Loughs), plants like the yellow-flowered slender St John's wort (*Hypericum pulchrum*) are found in the grassland. In places marsh lousewort (*Pedicularis palustris*) and the unusual (and unobtrusive) fern, moonwort (*Botrychium lunaria*) can be located. A heavily grazed 'blue' grassland zone is found in slightly drier lakeside (as at Lough Muckanagh). The blue colour is attributable to carnation sedge (*Carex panicea*). In places where the grassland is subject to pronounced fluctuations in the water table a plant association which includes silverweed and common sedge (*Carex nigra*) occurs.

The constantly wet fringes of this lake system have dominant communities of emergent plants – plants such as reeds which root in the lake bed but which rise above the water surface. A common association along the edges of the permanent water are rushes giving way to sedges and reeds in deeper water. In places there is an association of reeds and tussocks of club-rushes (*Scirpus*): in others tall sedge swamp and black bog-rush (*Schoenus nigricans*) combine. Stands of saw sedge (*Cladium*) well-named for its potential to lacerate unprotected flesh, cover acre upon acre of these shallow lakes (as at the western end of Lough Bunny). The insect-trapping (and digesting) bladderwort (*Utricularia*) is a common underwater associate of the stands of sedge but it usually goes unnoticed except when it extends its golden-yellow flowers above the water surface in late summer.

Pale butterwort.

The open water has beautiful and interesting flowers as well. Some of the turlough-type lakes, like Lough Cooloorta have the adaptable, amphibious bistort (*Polygonum amphibium*). Like the pondweeds it has floating leaves but its bright pink flower spikes are quite singular. Water crowfoot (*Ranunculus aquatilis*), so called because of its branched underwater leaves, has floating leaves which resemble those of a buttercup but white flowers which protrude above the water surface. Finest of all the open water plants are the water lilies. The white water lily (*Nymphaea alba*) has a white, yellow-centred flower which looks as fragile as egg-shell china: the yellow water lily (*Nuphar lutea*) has a bulbous flower cup of the deepest yellow. Both have large floating leaves which can prevent sunlight penetrating the sheltered backwaters in which they occur, often in abundance. They are found mainly in the deeper parts of some of the lakes, up to 2 metres (6.5 feet)

The uniqueness of the Burren flora

The Burren region demonstrates convincingly the potential for flowering profusion in circumstances where physical and chemical conditions are highly conducive to growth. It is, however, the mixture of plant assemblages or communities rather than the sheer abundance of species that makes the region unique. Plants normally found in regions as far apart as the Arctic and the Mediterranean occur together in the Burren. Some which have a distinctly Atlantic distribution grow beside others which are usually associated with alpine meadows. To complicate the matter further, plants which would normally be thought of as upland or montane species occur almost at sea level in places and alongside coastal plants. Moreover, plants which are normally found in woodlands grow in the open or in the limestone where there is no sign of tree cover.

The dense-flowered orchid is a Mediterranean plant which (with the exception of a few other localities) is not found anywhere else in northern Europe apart from the Burren. Its existence in the Burren can only be explained by a process of northward spread after the last retreat of the ice and subsequent isolation in a highly suitable habitat. Several of the other orchids, notably the pyramidal, the fly, the bee and the autumn lady's tresses must have arrived by the same process given their decidedly southern propensity. Certain other Burren plants have southern affinities and probably spread to Ireland in warmer ancient times. The maidenhair fern is one of the famous

---

BOX 7

Lusitanian plants of the Burren

The term Lusitanian is often applied to a group of plants which have their origins in the Iberian peninsula, particularly in Portugal and western Spain. They occur predominantly along the western European seaboards and are described as having 'Atlantic' affinities. A common Burren example is the pale butterwort (*Pinguicula lusitanica*) but there are a number of well known examples including the following:

tutsan	(*Hypericum androsaemum*)
navelwort	(*Umbilicus rupestris*)
wild madder	(*Rubia peregrina*)

The pteridophyte hay-scented buckler fern (*Dryopteris aemula*) is also classified as Lusitanian. A number of the Burren's shore plants are similarly classified including:

rock samphire	(*Crithmum maritimum*)
sea spurge	(*Euphorbia paralias*)
Portland spurge	(*Euphorbia portlandica*)

---

examples. Another is arguably the Burren's most beautiful flower, the large-flowered butterwort (*Pinguicula grandiflora*). Apart from its many localities in west Munster it is found nowhere else in north-western Europe. Pale butterwort (*Pinguicula lusitanica*) has a much less restricted distribution outside the Burren, but as an example of a lusitanian plant (distributed mainly along the Atlantic seaboard) shares a similar inability to cope with cold northern conditions as the real southerners.

Northern plants (those with a decidedly northern bias in their distribution-frost tolerant species) are represented in the Burren by the frog orchid (*Coeloglossum viride*) and the mossy saxifrage (*Saxifraga hypnoides*) among others. They owe their existence in the Burren today to a southward spread in colder times. Arctic plants are defined as those which grow on mountains in northern Europe and down to sea level in the Arctic. An example which has been found (though not recently) in the Burren is the arctic sandwort (*Arenaria norvegica*). Alpine species, on the other hand, are plants that grow primarily on the Alps. The well-known example is the spring gentian (*Gentiana verna*). Arctic-alpines are plants which are found both on lowland tundra in the Arctic and on the alpine massif. The only example found in the Burren is the mountain avens (*Dryas octopetala*) which is an abundant feature of the open limestone in mid summer.

Burren Specialities

There are about 25 really special Burren plants which are special not because of their beauty (though some most definitely are beautiful) but rather because of their rarity or their uniqueness in the country. Only two are so rare as to be found nowhere else in Ireland – the hoary rock-rose (*Helianthemum canum*) and a sea lavender (*Limonium* sp.) (purple milk-vetch (*Astragalus danicus*) is found only on the Aran Islands, not in the Burren). The pyramidal bugle (*Ajuga pyramidalis*), once thought to be confined to the Burren has been found since elsewhere, including on Rathlin Island in County Antrim.

The spring gentian is a flower of the 'western limestones' occurring in isolated pockets as for north as Mayo and widely in south Galway as well as in the Burren proper. In the Burren, however, it attains a singular abundance making it the obvious motif of the region's flora. Indeed it is as common in places as many of the standard 'weeds' like daisies and dandelions. The mountain avens is similarly (but more widely) distributed on the limestones, extending as far north as Fermanagh. It is also found as a montane plant on the cliffs and summits of some of the country's higher mountains. In the Burren it grows in super abundance both as a limestone pavement and as a montane species. It shares the pavement with the hoary rock-rose which has a highly restricted range being confined more or less to south-west Galway (including the Aran Islands) and north Clare. In places like Poulsallagh in the south-western Burren it covers acres of the rocky terrain – a floral display unique to these islands.

Other range-restricted calcicoles (plants which thrive on limy soils) such as many of the orchids and limestone grasses are, in general, ostentatiously abundant in the Burren.

The shrubby cinquefoil is found on the shore and on

Above: pyramidal bugle.
Centre: spring gentians.
Below: hoary rock-rose.

BOX 8

Special Burren plants:

The following is a list of plants whose national 'headquarters' are in the Burren. In some of these cases the Burren is their main area in the whole of Britain and Ireland and one or two are virtually unknown elsewhere in north-western Europe:

Hard shield fern	(*Polystichum aculeatum*)
Brittle bladder fern	(*Cystopteris fragilis*)
Maidenhair fern	(*Adiantum capillus-veneris*) (HQ. Brit. Isles)
Mountain avens	(*Dryas octopetala*) (HQ.Brit. Isles)
Irish eyebright	(*Euphrasia salisburgensis*) (HQ.Brit.Isles)
Spring gentian	(*Gentiana verna*) (HQ.Brit.Isles)
Dense-flowered orchid	(*Neotinea maculata*) (HQ.Brit.Isles)
Thyme broomrape	(*Orobanche alba*) (HQ.Brit.Isles)
Shrubby cinquefoil	(*Potentilla fruticosa*) (HQ.Brit.Isles)
Fen/turlough violet	(*Viola persicifolia*) (HQ. Brit.Isles)
Squinancywort	(*Asperula cynanchica*)
Field mouse-ear	(*Cerastium arvense*)
Dark-red helleborine	(*Epipactis atrorubens*)
Limestone bedstraw	(*Galium sterneri*)
Bloody cranesbill	(*Geranium sanguineum*)
Mudwort	(*Limosella aquatica*)
Spring sandwort	(*Minuartia verna*)
Stone bramble	(*Rubus saxatilis*)
Mossy saxifrage	(*Saxifraga hypnoides*)
Blue moor-grass	(*Sesleria albicans*)

Fen/turlough violet.

Thyme broomrape.

Irish eyebright.

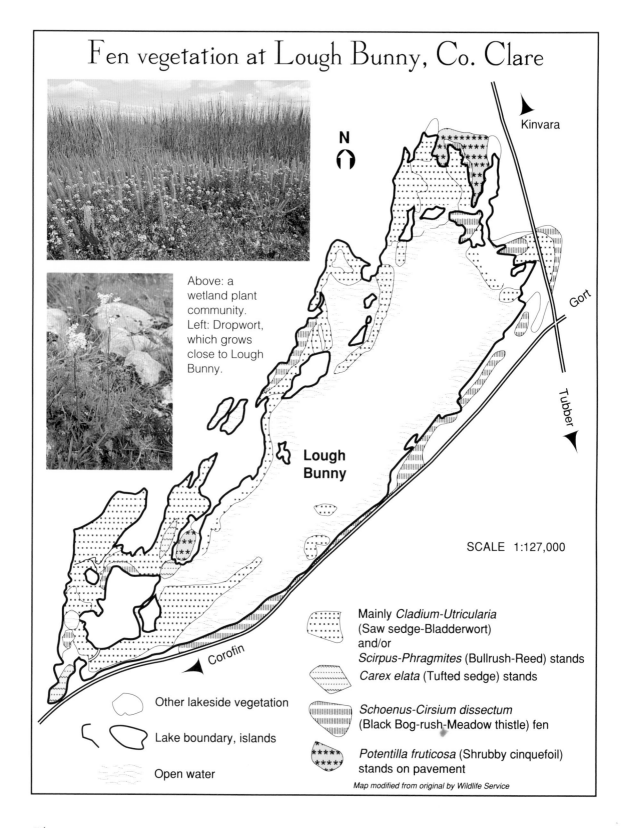

Fen vegetation at Lough Bunny, Co. Clare

N

Kinvara

Gort

Tubber

Above: a
wetland plant
community.
Left: Dropwort,
which grows
close to Lough
Bunny.

**Lough
Bunny**

Corofin

SCALE 1:127,000

Mainly *Cladium-Utricularia*
(Saw sedge-Bladderwort)
and/or
Scirpus-Phragmites (Bullrush-Reed) stands

Carex elata (Tufted sedge) stands

Schoenus-Cirsium dissectum
(Black Bog-rush-Meadow thistle) fen

Potentilla fruticosa (Shrubby cinquefoil)
stands on pavement

Other lakeside vegetation

Lake boundary, islands

Open water

Map modified from original by Wildlife Service

some of the islands of Lough Corrib, besides many of the turloughs of the Burren. Around one or two of the turloughs it grows so densely as to inhibit access. This circumstance is unique – the plant is found only in a few places in Britain and indeed north-western Europe. Another turlough flower, the turlough violet (also called the fen violet), though known from a number of other Irish counties has its centre of distribution in the turloughs of the Clare/Galway border region.

In Britain it has declined to the verge of extinction due to drainage activities. Dropwort is also confined, in Ireland, to a small district in the Clare/Galway border region where it grows in abundance (e.g. on the broken limestone of the Gort lowlands).

Quite a few of these plants, besides being regional specialities, are so familiar as to rank among the most striking representatives of all the flowers. Mountain avens, for instance, with its eight creamy petals, its contrasting dark upper and pale lower sides to its leaves and its woody stems, is a regional favourite. So too is the spring gentian, which although small and unusually formed must surely be bluer than anything else that grows. The mossy and the Irish saxifrages (*Saxifraga rosacea*) look quite alike and grow together in places in the north-western Burren: they make wonderful photographic subjects in their natural setting. It may be necessary to use a range of techniques including flash to photograph some of the crevice-dwelling plants like the mosses and the ferns. Maidenhair fern, for instance, is found mainly in dark, damp situations.

The importance of cherishing this flora cannot be overstated. In the past, samples of the flowers were collected by visitors, unaware of their scarcity: nowadays people come to look, photograph or sketch and depart with memories rather than mementos.

Top: shrubby cinquefoil.
Centre: Irish saxifrage.
Below: large-flowered butterwort.

Fauna

Invertebrates

$\mathcal{M}$ost books on natural history are either involved deeply in invertebrates – i.e. they allocate to them their rightful significance in the ecosystem, for they are more populous than other animal forms – or tend to play them down. This book proposes neither approach. It is essential if the book is to deal with the fauna of the Burren adequately that it alludes to those groups of organisms which the would-be naturalist is likely to encounter, but does so without involving the reader in intricate tedium. So numerous, however, are the genera (never mind the species) that it is difficult to discuss them at all without becoming lost in a wilderness of scientific nomenclature and minuscule detail.

This text has concentrated on the most widespread examples likely to be encountered, but consideration has also been given to some invertebrates which have a particular importance in the context of the Burren. While the unobtrusive have not been forgotten completely, emphasis is naturally placed on the larger or more showy invertebrates, like the butterflies.

Invertebrates are a massive classification of animals with tens of thousands of species which are classified into discrete groups. The group Protista conveniently encompasses invisible, single-celled organisms like Foraminifera – among the simplest and most ancient of life forms on the planet. These primitive organisms exist in free-living masses in fresh and salt water and provide food for a myriad higher forms of zooplankton.

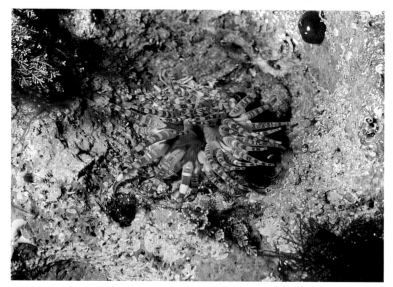

Coelenterata is a group that contains such familiar animals as sea anemones and jellyfish. Common examples like the ruby-red beadlet anemone (*Actinia equina*) and the velvet-green snakelocks anemone (*Anemonia viridis*) can be seen in the rock pools at Black Head and

Gem anemone.

Carrickadda. The best-known jellyfish are the moon jelly (*Aurelia aurita*) and the aptly named compass jellyfish (*Chrysaora hysoscella*). The radiating brown lines on its surface resemble those on the dial of a ship's compass. A strange relative of the jellyfish, the by-the-wind sailor (*Velella velella*) – a mini-jellyfish with a sail! – has occasionally been cast ashore along the Clare coast more than a thousand miles north of its usual tropical home.

Compass jellyfish.

Echinoderms include such well-known marine creatures as starfish (Asteroidea), brittle-stars (Ophiuroidea) and sea urchins (Echinoidea). Purple sea urchins (*Paracentrotus lividus*) are found in colonies along the rocky coast. At Black Head they can be seen inside the little cup-shaped depressions which they excavate for their own protection. Occasionally their remarkably etched tests (shells) or those of the sea potato (*Echinocardium cordatum*) are washed up on the shore: they make beautiful ornaments.

Annelida is the group containing worms and their allies.

Eroded rock pools formed by a colony of purple sea urchins.

In the Rine saltmarsh both lugworms (*Arenicola*) and ragworms (*Nereis*) inhabit the mudflats where they are as eagerly sought by fishermen as they are by the wading birds found there. At low tide near the outfall of the Caher river, a large colony of honeycomb worms (*Sabellaria alveolata*) is exposed. The colonial home is, as the name suggests, in the form of a massive honeycomb, though marvellously constructed from sand particles

and not wax. Only when the tide covers the colony do the worms partially emerge to feed on plankton.

One of the largest invertebrate groups is the molluscs. They are found both on land and in water-in fresh and in salt. Examples like those which lived in the sea in the Carboniferous era are still found in the sea off the Burren coast today. They include bivalves like cockles, mussels, scallops and oysters. The Gastropods (spiral-shells) include winkles and whelks. Factors such as tolerance to exposure result in the zonation of periwinkles (*Littorina*) from the upper to the lower levels of the intertidal area of the shore – in a similar manner to that of the brown seaweeds. Some of the mollusc shells are highly decorative. One of the finest (but smallest) is the European cowrie (*Trivia monacha*) which can be picked up occasionally along the Flaggy shore. Many of the cobble-sized limestones washed up on the shore or thrown up into the dry stone walls are heavily pitted with thumb-sized holes. This is the work of the rock-borer (*Hiatella*), a bivalve mollusc. Like the purple sea urchin it excavates its sanctuary but instead of secreting acid it wears away at the rock with a serrated edge on its shell. A possible link between the shore snails (periwinkles) and those of the land, was found in the form of a rare terrestrial species (*Pomatias elegans*), discovered at Finavarra in 1976.

Land snails are extremely abundant in the Burren. Dozens of species are represented, from the familiar garden snail (*Helix aspersa*) to the various banded snails (*Cepaea*). The shells of the latter can be found smashed in heaps beside a rock where some scrub-dwelling song thrush has opened them. On hot summer days the Burren's snails retreat to the grikes where they can find moisture in the moss cushions. They can be seen to their best

Top left: granular abstract – communal home of honeycomb worm. Left: pock-marked limestone – the work of a rock boring mollusc.

advantage in wet weather when they emerge *en masse* to feed. Their striped spiral shells are often as pleasing to the eye as the plants on which they feed. Enormous numbers of snails (particularly *H. aspersa*) are found on Deer Island where they feed voraciously on the salt-tolerant plants.

As most freshwater snails cannot tolerate complete drying, true turloughs are not important snail habitats. In the fenny turloughs or in circumstances where there is some fluctuation in water level, freshwater snails abound. They are mainly the thin-shelled *Lymnaea* and the flat spiralled *Planorbis* but occasional orb shells (*Sphaerium corneum*) occur too, looking like miniature fresh-water cockles.

The arthropods form the largest animal group, containing myriapods (centipedes and millipedes), crustaceans (crabs, shrimps etc.), arachnids (spiders) and of course insects. Myriapods are relatively unimportant in the context of the Burren for they are invertebrates of decaying leaf litter and similar compost-like habitats. The fact that only a few of the many Irish species are found in the region is probably a reflection of the lack of this kind of habitat. They are most often found in the organic soils and litter in the damper parts of the hazel scrub.

Banded snail on grass stem.

Crustaceans, on the other hand, are well represented on the land, in freshwater and along the coast. At least seven species of woodlouse occur, with *Trichoniscus* common and widespread. The sea slater (*Ligia oceanica*) is the shoreline counterpart of the terrestrial woodlouse and is equally common. The freshwater has a variety of crustaceans like water fleas (*Daphnia*) which are particularly abundant. Fresh water shrimps (*Gammarus*) are common in the lake systems and turloughs. A regional speciality, the fairy shrimp (*Tanymastix stagnalis*), was first recorded for Britain and Ireland in Rahasane turlough. It has since been found in several of the Burren's turloughs. The coastal crustaceans are nowhere better represented than at Carrickadda. Here barnacles of several species share the rocky reef with molluscs like limpets. There is a wonderful variety among the crabs and their relatives. Besides the better-known shore crab (*Carcinus maenas*) and the edible crab (*Cancer pagurus*) there are the velvet swimming crab (*Liocarcinus puber*), porcelain crabs (*Porcellana* spp.), spider crabs and occasional squat lobsters (Anomura). Squat lobsters are also found in the submarine caves along the Burren's western seaboard.

Limpet grazing marks on algae coated boulder.

Arachnids are mainly spiders, mites and ticks. About a dozen spiders are known to be common on the limestone with a further 15 in the dunes at Fanore. They belong to several groups: tube-weavers, night-hunters, wolf, orb-webs and jumping spiders among others. Three species are dominant on the open limestone including the dark and fearsome-looking *Segestria senoculata* – one of the tube-weavers which hunts by lying in wait in a tube-shaped cobweb sanctuary. The night-hunting spiders *Drassodes*, *Dysdera* and *Clubiona* are also widespread. *Dysdera*, a brick-red spider which hides under stones during the day, is an avid night-time hunter of the Burren's woodlice. The typically slim, athletic-looking wolf spiders (*Lycosa*) are widespread day time hunters. The orb-webs are common in low vegetation where they spin their elaborate webs. A typical Burren orb-web is the stout-bodied garden spider (*Araneus*). The tiny, 6mm (0.25 in) jumping spider (*Heliophanus*) which has the jumping capability of grasshopper is easily recognised by its bright greenish yellow palps. Some rare or unusual spiders such as *Entelecara errata*, which is known elsewhere as a rare mountain spider, have been found in the Burren.

Harvestmen, those 'daddy-long-legs' spiders are common in the open Burren and on the hazel scrub-floor. They (and other invertebrates) are sometimes parasitised by tiny red mites-also arachnids. Soft-bodied red mites are remarkably common in the open karst, their pin head-sized scarlet bodies standing out vividly against the grey limestone.

Insects

This is the best-known invertebrate group, and includes flies, beetles, aphids, bees, butterflies and moths, bugs, dragonflies and others. Much has been discovered about the Burren's insects over the past few decades.

Due to concentrated work by entomologists a great deal has been discovered about the Lepidoptera (butterflies and moths) which suggests that the Burren is a most important habitat for them. Were it possible to deduce that these showy creatures are representative of the Burren's insects as a whole then the conservation of the region would be justifiable on this basis alone. However, as other forms are less obvious and therefore less well known it is not possible to make this deduction at this stage.

The water bugs of the turloughs have been investigated. Their descriptive names give a clue to their often bizarre appearance and their strictly aquatic way of life. Water boatmen (*Notonecta* spp.), water measurers (*Hydrometra stagnorum*), water crickets (*Velis* spp.), pond skaters (*Gerris* spp.) and water scorpions (*Nepa cinerea*) are widespread turlough inhabitants. Together with water beetles (Corixidae) and a variety of fly nymphs they form important food for wintering wildfowl. This diversity is not reflected on the Aran Islands (with the exception of one or two of the larger turloughs), suggesting the problems which habitat-specific creatures face in expanding their ranges. The lack of mayfly (Ephemera) and stonefly (Plecoptera) larvae on the islands despite their abundance in the Burren further illustrates this point.

Dragonflies (Anisoptera) and damselflies (Zygoptera) are common and widespread especially in the eastern Burren wetlands where they feed on ubiquitous midges and mosquitoes. There are probably more than the 14 species recorded by An Foras Forbartha (1978) though only about a dozen are common. The dragon-flies are sub divided into the hawkers (those that fly and hover a lot) and the darters (those that dart out from a resting place to catch their prey by ambush). The common aeshna (*Aeshna juncea*) is a familiar sight in the fenny turloughs in mid-summer. The brown aeshna (*Aeshna grandis*), our largest dragonfly, can be seen more commonly in the autumn and often well away from water, in the hazel scrub. The darter dragonflies are less attractive than the hawkers. They are represented by the family Libellulidae. The four-spotted libellula (*L. quadrimaculata*) in its nymphal stage is a well-known part of the benthic fauna of the turloughs.

The constant buzz of grasshoppers (Acrididae) is a feature of the unfertilised meadowland of the Burren. Several species are found, including the field grasshopper (*Chorthippus brunneus*). There is great variation in colour and in habitat, making identifi-cation of most species difficult.

Beetles (Coleoptera) are represented by groups which in-clude the ground beetles (Carabidae), rove beetles (Staphylinidae), chafers (Scarabaeidae), soldiers (Cantharidae), ladybirds (Coccinellidae), leaf beetles (Chrysomelidae) and weevils (Curculionidae). Of the large ground beetles the inch-long *Carabus*

Common *Sympetrum* dragonfly.

Rose chafer on burnet rose.

nemoralis with its bronze-black body is widespread in the lime-stone. Ground beetles are also associated with the turloughs. Having hibernated 'in the dry' above the high water mark the beetles follow the receding wa-ter table to hunt for crustacea and insect larvae left high and dry. Two rare beetles which specialise in this carniverous ex-ploitation are *Agonum livens* and *Badister meridionatis*. Chafers, particularly the rose chafer (*Cetonia aurata*), are associated

with some of the Burren plants like the burnet rose. On sunny summer days they can be seen feeding on the petals, their shiny green wing-cases glinting in the sun. Weevils are distinguished from other beetles by their long pointed snouts; 20 have been recorded at Mullaghmore, and 12 at the Fanore dunes. Three of the six Irish species of bagous weevils have been found in the Burren.

As anyone who has sat down only to get up again quickly from a thyme-covered mound will testify, the Burren has a myriad colonies of ants (Formicidae). Both the black ant (*Lasius niger*) and the yellow ant (*Lasius flavus*) are common.

With such an abundance of scented flowers, pollinating insects are everywhere to be seen throughout the summer. Hoverflies (Syrphidae), many looking like miniature wasps, have a crucial role in the process. Many are represented: occasional rarities like *Cheilosia laskai* have been identified too. Wild bumble bees (Bombidae) are common with both social and solitary types represented. Bumble bees are readily distinguished by their stout bodies and black, orange or yellow body fur. Honey bees (*Apis mellifera*) on the other hand are generally blackish and smaller. In the Burren they are the progeny of escaped bees from apiaries. Colonies were recorded in limestone crevices by Stelfox in 1924 and by Brinklow and Nash 50 years later. Wasps are also composed of social and solitary species, though there are proportionately less of each compared with the bees. The papery-looking nests of social wasps have been found in the roof spaces of old disused buildings in the Burren.

Grey dagger moth on a drystone wall.

Moths

Thanks to the dedicated work of E. S. A. Baynes and more recently R. F. Haynes, much light has been shone upon the nocturnal Lepidoptera. The mercury-vapour lamp which attracts these insects like nothing else can has shown that perhaps half of the 540 or so Irish moths are found in the Burren.

Many are common and widespread resident species, including the noctuid moths whose generally cryptic colour and pattern permits them to rest during the day, camouflaged against the surface of wood or stone. The grey dagger (*Acronicta psi*) and the herald (*Scoliopteryx libatrix*) are representatives of this group. The more striking tiger and ermine moths (Arctiidae) are often attracted to lamps at night. The caterpillars of the drinker (*Philudoria potatoria*) and the oak eggar (*Lasiocampa quercus*) are commonly found in the open Burren during the autumn suggesting the abundance of these heavily built insects. Y moths, so called because of the clear Y-shaped mark on their closed wings, have been identified also. One of these, the silver Y (*Autographa gamma*) is a migrant from southern Europe usually found in the Burren in the latter summer. Other migrant moths recorded in the Burren include the rusty dot (*Pyrausta martialis*), the rush veneer (*Nomophila noctuella*) and the great brocade (*Eurois occulta*).

Some of that spectacular group of moths, the hawkmoths (Sphingidae) also migrate to Ireland (and the Burren) including the convolvulus hawkmoth (*Agrius convolvuli*)-a massive greyish insect – and the remarkable hummingbird hawkmoth

Narrow-bordered bee hawkmoth larvae.

(*Macroglossum stellatarum*) which closely resembles a small humming bird. The narrow-bordered bee hawkmoth (*Hemaris tityus*) looks much more like a bee than a day-flying moth. It occurs locally in the wet pastureland of the eastern Burren. The scrubland along the eastern Burren is a good place to look for the beautiful emperor moth (*Saturnia pavonia*) in spring. The males with their rufous-tinted rear wings can be seen in flight during the day looking for females which they can sense with their elaborate antennae.

The Burren turns up rarities too, particularly among the numerous micro-moths, like the insignificant-looking *Alucita icterodactyla*, which was discovered in the Burren in 1952 and was otherwise unknown in Ireland or in Britain. The most famous though, is the Burren green (*Calamia tridens o.*) which, until it was discovered there in 1949 was also unknown from Ireland and Britain. It is the source of some amazement that this beautiful lime-green, inch-long moth which is locally abundant in the Burren could have remained there undetected until so recently. Its larvae can be found on grasses in and around Ballyvaughan.

More than a dozen day-flying (diurnal) moths are common in the Burren in summer. The most eye-catching are the burnets (Zygaenidae) with their striking black, red-spotted wings. The six-spot burnet (*Zygaena filipendulae*) and the transparent burnet (*Z. purpuralis*) are the family representatives – the latter is a source of excitement to visiting naturalists who know of it only as a rarity in England. The cinnabar (*Tyria jacobaeae*), though

Left: six-spot burnet.
Above: transparent burnet.
Opposite: the Burren green moth
– unknown elsewhere in Ireland
or Britain.

largely nocturnal and unrelated, has a similar red and black wing pattern to the burnets and may be encountered in the region in broad daylight. Very common diurnal moths in the high summer are the unobtrusive chimney sweeper (*Odezia atrata*), the speckled yellow (*Pseudopanthera macularia*), the common heath (*Ematurga atomaria*) and the burnet companion (*Euclidia glyphica*). Care needs to be taken in the identification of this last moth for it can look like one of the Burren's more dowdy butterflies – the dingy skipper.

Butterflies

Of the diverse wildlife with which the Burren is endowed the butterflies are decidedly one of its most remarkable features. People who are attracted to the region in the summer to admire the flowers invariably allude to the butterflies and wonder at their role in the natural equilibrium of the place.

Ireland has a mere 34 species (compared to more than 60 in Britain.) Of these, 29 are resident and the other five are migrants or rare visitors. At least 30 species have been recorded in the Burren (more than anywhere else in the country), and 26 of these are resident. Butterflies are, in fact, equally valid symbols of the Burren's richness and colour as are the flowers.

Many of the Lepidoptera found in the region are common species which are widespread throughout Ireland. Those like the whites (Pieridae) – the large, small, green-veined and orange-tip – or the browns (Satyridae) – the meadow, wall, ringlet and

Resident Butterflies of

Small tortoiseshell (*Aglais urticae*)

Brimstone (*Gonepteryx rhamni*)

Peacock (*Inachis io*)

Holly blue (*Celastrina argiolus*)

Orange tip (*Anthocharis cardamines*)

Speckled wood (*Pararge aegeria*)

Green-veined white (*Pieris napi*)

Small white (*Pieris rapae*)

Large white (*Pieris brassicae*)

Wall (*Lasiommata megera*)

Green hairstreak (*Callophrys rubi*)

Wood white (*Leptidea sinapis*)

Dingy skipper(*Erynnis tages*)

Pearl-bordered fritillary (*Boloria euphrosyne*)

Small heath (*Coenonympha pamphilus*)

Common blue (*Polyommatus icarus*)

Small blue (*Cupido minimus*)

Marsh fritillary (*Eurodryas aurinia*)

Meadow brown (*Maniola jurtina*)

Ringlet (*Aphantopus hyperantus*)

Dark green fritillary (*Argynnis aglaja*)

Grayling (*Hipparchia semele*)

Silver-washed fritillary (*Argynnis paphia*)

Brown hairstreak (*Thecla betulae*)

BURREN BUTTERFLY CALENDAR
(Normal annual flying period for adult butterflies

Butterflies	January	February	March	April	May
Speckled Wood				W	▬
Wall Brown					W ▬
Grayling					
Meadow Brown					
Small Heath					▸
Ringlet					
Pearl-Bordered Fritillary					▬
Dark Green Fritillary					
Silver-washed Fritillary					
Marsh Fritillary					▬
Small Tortoiseshell	▬ ▬ ▬ ▬ ▬	▬ ▬ ▬ ▬ ▬	▬ ▬ ▬ ▬ H	W	▬
Peacock	▬ ▬ ▬ ▬ ▬	▬ ▬ ▬ ▬ ▬	▬ ▬ ▬ ▬ H	W	▬
Small Blue					▸
Common Blue					▸
Holly Blue				S	▬
Small Copper					
Green Hairstreak					S ▬
Brown Hairstreak					
Wood White					W ▬
Large White					W ▬
Small White				W	▬
Green-veined White				W	▬
Orange Tip				W	▬
Brimstone	▬ ▬ ▬ ▬ ▬	▬ ▬ ▬ ▬ ▬	▬ ▬ ▬ ▬ H	W	▬
Dingy Skipper					▸
Red Admiral					M ▬
Painted Lady					▸

Status in the Burren
W : widespread
S : scarce or local
M : migrant
H : hibernation

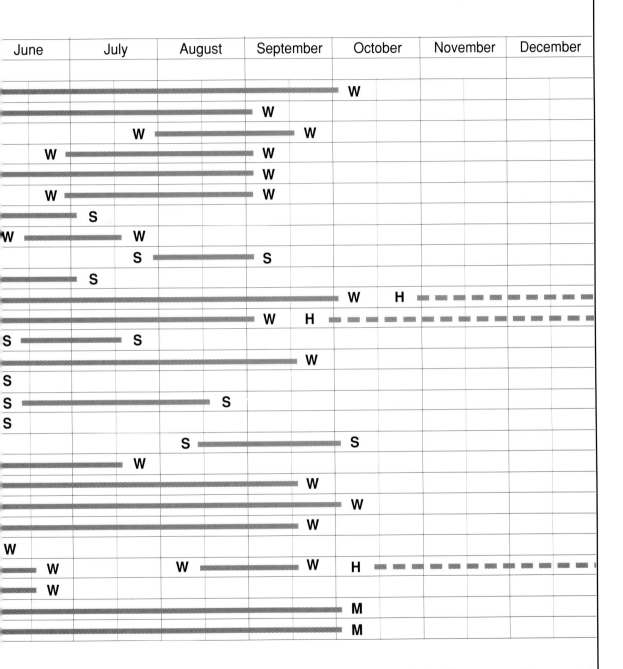

This chart is based on observation in the Burren over a 5 year period
and covers the resident species and commonest migrants.

speckled wood – for instance are common throughout the country. Attractive, eye-catching species like the common blue (*Polyommatus icarus*), small tortoiseshell (*Aglais urticae*), small copper (*Lycaena phlaeas*) and peacock (*Inachis io*) are also widely distributed.

But the Burren also boasts four fritillary butterflies – the silver-washed, the dark-green, the marsh and the pearl-bordered – none of which is particularly common nationally and two (the latter two) of which are extremely local. In fact, the pearl-bordered fritillary (*Boloria euphrosyne*) is found nowhere else in Ireland. Its highly restricted range is suggestive of the past arborial cover of the Burren for this is a woodland butterfly elsewhere in Europe. The brown hairstreak (*Thecla betulae*) is also more or less restricted to north Clare and south-east Galway.

A few butterflies are found locally elsewhere in Ireland, (on eskers, sand dunes etc.) but are widespread and abundant in the Burren. These include the small blue (*Cupido minimus*) the dingy skipper (*Erynnis tages*), the brimstone (*Gonepteryx rhamni*) and the grayling (*Hipparchia semele*). Other interesting and local butterflies are the wood white (*Leptidea sinapis*) and the holly blue (*Celastrina argiolus*), both of which suggest, along with the pearl-bordered fritillary, former woodland cover.

The food plants of the larvae of many of these butterflies are calcicoles, which helps to explain their abundance. The wide range of grasses provide feeding for the caterpillars of many of the brown butterflies and the small heath (*Coenonympha pamphilus*). That typical close-growing Burren flower, bird's foot trefoil (*Lotus corniculatus*), hosts the caterpillars of the common blue, while kidney vetch (*Anthyllis vulneraria*) patches are the places to look for the small blue. Two lime-loving shrubs the buckthorn (*Rhamnus catharticus*) and the blackthorn (*Prunus spinosa*) host the brimstone and the brown hairstreak respectively.

As with the moths, the Burren attracts its share of migrant butterflies. The commonest is the red admiral (*Vanessa atalanta*) which occurs more or less annually and in some years, when there is a protracted southerly airstream, it is quite common. Painted lady butterflies (*Cynthia cardui*) are regular late summer migrants to the south and east coasts of Ireland but are scarce in the Burren. In some years, clouded yellows (*Colias croceus*), mustard-yellow migrants from the Mediterranean, are also seen. Ireland's rarest resident butterfly the purple hairstreak (*Quercusia quercus*) was more

---

BOX 9

Butterflies with distinct Irish sub-species

The following butterflies found in the Burren are Irish sub-species and are recognisably different from their counterparts found in Britain.

Meadow brown (*Maniola jurtina iernes*). The Irish race is larger in both male and female with a brighter upper-wing pattern (more orange in the wing of the female in particular).

Orange tip (*Anthocharis cardamines hibernica*). The hind wing (upper wing) of the female is yellowish, unlike the British race.

Common blue (*Polyommatus icarus mariscolore*). The Irish race is larger and a brighter blue than the British.

Wood white (*Leptidea sinapis juvernica*). In the male the undersides of the rear wings are shaded olive green not pale grey as in the British race.

Marsh fritillary (*Eurodryas aurinia hibernica*).

or less unknown in the west of Ireland until it was seen in Garryland wood in 1988 – a suggestion perhaps, that the region holds more butterfly secrets than it has so far revealed.

Vertebrates

Fish, amphibians and reptiles

Consideration of the fishlife of such a waterless place as the Burren would appear to be an unnecessary exercise. However, as the region incorporates the north Clare coastline and the freshwater wetlands of the Galway/Clare border, it warrants some comment.

Tourist signs along the north-west coastline of the Burren give an indication of the fish species which are commonly caught by sea anglers and the fact that international contests are held there is an indication of their abundance and diversity. They include pollack (*Pollachius*), ling (*Molva*), cod (*Gadus*), wrasse (*Labrus*), bearded rockling (*Ciliata*), whiting (*Merlangius*), ray (*Raja*), dogfish (*Scyliorhinus*) and conger (*Conger*). Good-sized bass (*Dicentrarchus*) are still caught in the breaking surf on Fanore beach. In the rock pools and amongst the weed at low tide are gobys (*Gobius*) and blennys (*Blennius*) too small to catch by hook and often overlooked because of their camouflage patterns. Herring (*Clupea*) and mackerel (*Scomber*) are most abundant in shoals to-

Basking shark inshore at Fanore – once numerous, now noteworthy.

wards the end of summer. The latter are caught traditionally with feathered hooks in Galway Bay. The Aran Islanders subsisted for centuries on the rich fishing grounds between the islands and the Burren coastline. More recently deep-sea fishing has become a popular leisure activity. A number of shark species have been caught including some specimen porbeagles (*Lamna*). Large tope (*Galeorhinus*) are also caught in Galway Bay. Participants at the

Burren Symposium (May, 1988) were treated to close views of a basking shark (*Cetorhinus*) which spent several days patrolling the Burren coastline at Fanore in harmless pursuit of its staple diet, plankton.

No doubt the rich concentration of fish here is a factor in the healthy common seal population in the Bay, the steadily increasing cormorant colony on Deer island (170 pairs in 1971-300 pairs in 1989) and the hundreds of divers which obtain winter sustenence in the Bay and along the Burren's north coast.

Freshwater Fish

Three-spined stickleback (*Gasterosteus*) and eels (*Anguilla*) are so common as to be found in virtually all permanent or semi-permanent bodies of water in the region, both large and small. Pike (*Esox*), perch (*Perca*), rudd (*Scardinius*) and bream (*Abramis*) are found in the lakes of the freshwater system along the Burren's eastern boundary. These coarse fish are thought to have been introduced or to have invaded the lakes from the river outfall to the south, for they are not regarded as native. Tench (*Tinca*) (a recent introduction from Britain) is known from some of the larger lakes in the system. Loughs George, Muckanagh and Bunny (apparently, though not visibly) discharge into the Fergus. They do not contain abundant game fish but sizable specimens have been caught in the past. Lake trout (*Salmo trutta*) of up to 900 grams (2 pounds) have been landed, as have large pike up to 9 kilograms (20 pounds). Loughs Inchiquin and Atedaun contain brown trout (*Salmo trutta*) and occasional salmon (*Salmo salar*). In fact salmon spawn as far up the Fergus as Corofin. Bream (of several kilograms) are known from Lough Inchiquin, and perch and rudd are also caught there in good numbers.

The importance of these lakes for fishing has been diminishing in recent years according to the fishermen who frequent the system. This has been attributed to pollution and particularly to silage run-off in the Corofin area.

Stocking is carried out by local fishing groups, who release game species into the Fergus below Corofin. Stocking has also been carried out on Lough Murree near New Quay. Rainbow (*Salmo gairdneri*) and brown trout were introduced here in 1975 but did not survive – probably because of the fluctuating salinity of the lake. The River Aille holds wild sea trout (*Salmo trutta*) and the Caher which flows out at Fanore probably produces them as well, for they are caught at the river outfall at Fanore beach. (A few only in recent years).

Brown trout in the Caher River.

Amphibians

Ireland has only three amphibians and two of these, the frog (*Rana*) and the common or smooth newt (*Triturus vulgaris*), are found in the Burren. The third, the natterjack toad (*Bufo calamita*) is restricted to County Kerry.

Despite its familiarity the frog is not native to Ireland and may have been introduced as late as the Middle Ages. It is nevertheless widespread today and though the Burren can be regarded as superficially one of the country's driest districts (and hence unsuitable), the frog may be encountered almost anywhere. The wetlands of the east Burren have abundant frog populations, while even the small turloughs and ponds hold a few. Their gelatinous grey masses of frogspawn are much in evidence even before spring is underway. By the time they have hatched out into tadpoles they are heavily predated by herons and otters. Otter spraints (droppings) comprised mainly of frog bones can be found along the lake shores between Corofin and Boston.

The common newt has a lifestyle similar to that of the frog. Hibernation sites, however, may be distant from the summer haunts and are usually under stones. They may be found in this situation lying torpid for the duration of the winter and looking like miniatuare rubber lizards from a child's 'lucky bag'. Stones concealing hibernating newts which are moved should be carefully replaced to allow them to complete their winter sleep. Their summer habitats are freshwater ponds and open wells. Many of the 'holy' wells with which the Burren is liberally endowed have resident populations of newts. Being small and having a tendency to stay below the water surface they are often overlooked. Even when the male dons his bright orange belly-flush and performs the elaborate nuptial display, newts may go unnoticed. Often their only contact with people is when they accidentally enter houses during their seasonal wanderings. They are often misidentified as lizards, but are regarded generally as a good omen by country folk.

Reptiles

The only reptile widely regarded as being native to the Burren (and Ireland) is the common or viviparous lizard (*Lacerta vivipara*). It gives birth to live young. Though it is widespread and locally common, few people are familiar with the lizard and some are not even aware that it occurs in this country. The

Common lizard.

reason for this lack of familiarity is that this little creature is unobtrusive and though it will bask in open sunny spots like other lizards, it disappears out of sight at the slightest hint of danger.

The lizard is especially common in the Burren, favouring sunny, windless places. There may be a connection between its haunts and the availability of its invertebrate food, for it is often to be found near ant colonies. In warm summer weather, it may be encountered scuttling across the green roads or hiding in dry-stone walls. The inner enclosures of the stone-built forts are sun-traps in summer and good places to look for lizards.

Though somewhat variable in colour and pattern the lizard is normally yellowish-brown or greyish with irregular blackish markings along the body length. Coloured thus, it is extremely difficult to see them on a moss- or lichen-covered background and usually the only glimpse is a fleeting one. The males are smaller than the females, averaging 13 centimetres (5 inches). Females may be up to 20 centimetres (7.8 inches) long.

In 1958, a number of green lizards (*Lacerta viridis*) were released into the Burren, and although they apparently died out without becoming established, at least one was reliably reported four years later. The green lizard is a much larger creature than our own, averaging some 40 centimetres (15.5 inches). It is hard to believe that, as an inhabitant of warmer countries adjoining the Mediterranean, it could survive (as it obviously did) for years in the relatively damp and cold west of Ireland. The same might be said of the slow worm (*Anguis fragilis*), a legless lizard, native to most of Europe (including Britain). This creature was first noticed in the Burren in the early 1970s, where it had apparently been

introduced at some stage previously. Several sightings were made in the Cappaghmore district, south-west of Kinvara, including some by a bulldozer driver who, in the course of clearing a field of rocks described encounters with 'snakes' (the slow-worm resembles a small, bronze-coloured snake). One was caught and submitted to University College Galway in 1977, where it was satisfactorily identified, and one was captured and photographed in spring, 1988. That the animal is surviving and thriving is without doubt for a young slow worm was found along with two adults later in 1988. It would appear that the slow worm is in the Burren to stay. To date, all the sightings have emanated from the north-eastern corner of the region, but it cannot be long before it colonises a good part of the wild rocky habitat, which it obviously finds to its liking.

Marine turtles (Cheloniidae) are little known from Ireland, being generally equatorial reptiles, but occasionally they turn up on our west coast, trans-

The slow worm – not a worm but a legless lizard.

ported there on the North Atlantic Drift. A few have been recorded along the Burren's coast.
A Ridley turtle (*Lepidochelys
kempi*), originating in the Gulf of
Mexico, has been found at
Milltown Malbay and there have
been other records from the west
of Ireland. The leatherback turtle (*Dermochelys coriacea*), also an
inhabitant of warm equatorial
Atlantic waters, was recorded at
Lahinch in July 1983. Others are
encountered annually at different locations along our Atlantic

Killeenaran's loggerhead turtle,
March 1990.

seaboard. Just how these enormous turtles (the size of an oval-
shaped dining room table) become so lost as to end up thousands
of miles off course is something of a mystery. Unfortunately they
often do, and end up ignominiously entangled in fishermen's nets
or washed up helpless on the shore.

After a protracted period of storms in February 1990 several
marine turtles turned up along the west coast of Ireland. One, a
metre-long (3.3 feet), 20-kilogram (44-pound) loggerhead turtle
(*Caretta c.*) was found washed up in inner Galway Bay, at
Killeenaran.

Birds

It is convenient to consider the Burren's birdlife by reference to
the three major habitat divisions into which the region can be divided: the limestone proper (with its features such as escarpments
and hazel scrub); the freshwater wetlands; and the coastline.

A male yellowhammer in song.

The birds of the limestone country

Overall, the open karst is not outstanding in terms of the
numbers or the diversity of the birds which are found there. In
fact, much of the rocky terrain is devoid of birds all year round,
except for open ground species like meadow pipits (*Anthus
pratensis*) and skylarks (*Alauda arvensis*). This paucity is particularly evident in winter when, apart from ravens (*Corvus corax*),
hooded crows (*Corvus corone*) and the odd small party of golden

plover (*Pluvialis apricaria*) (on the high plateau), around a dozen species is the likely tally in the course of a long walk. Most of the diversity is to be found near farmhouses or other 'abnormalities' in the topography. Here species like tits (Paridae), thrushes (Turdidae), finches (Fringillidae), including yellowhammers (*Emberiza citrinella*), magpies (*Pica p.*), redwings (*Turdus iliacus*) and fieldfares (*Turdus pilaris*), are to be expected. Snow buntings (*Plectrophenax nivalis*) occur in ones and twos during the winter months but mainly along or near the coast.

The hazel scrub conceals some surprises like the occasional snipe (*Gallinago g.*) and woodcock (*Scolopax rusticola*), but the diversity and abundance of bird species is no greater than would be found in neglected pasture with hedgerows elsewhere in Ireland. Robin (*Erithacus rubecula*), wren (*Troglodytes t.*), blue tit (*Parus caeruleus*) and chaffinch (*Fringilla coelebs*) have been found to be the commonest year-round residents in this habitat. Blackbird (*Turdus merula*) and dunnock (*Prunella modularis*), though widespread, are less common. The scrub provides an important sanctuary for our smallest bird, the goldcrest (*Regulus r.*), though to a minor degree only in summer.

Above : the wren – one of the Burren's commonest birds.
Below: male stonechat in typical pose.

Of the summer visitors the willow warbler (*Phylloscopus trochilus*) is the dominant species in the scrub but the whitethroat (*Sylvia communis*), having recovered from a population crash in the 1970s, is widespread in the haw and blackthorn thickets. Cuckoos (*Cuculus canorus*) are commoner in the open ground. The nightjar (*Caprimulgus europaeus*), one of the speciality summer visitors to the Burren is found in one or two of the less disturbed places. Another scarce summer visitor, the whinchat (*Saxicola rubetra*),

is found in one or two locations along the southern edge of the region while the resident stone-chat (*Saxicola torquata*), is commoner, particularly along the coast. Wheatears (*Oenanthe o.*) are a thinly scattered summer resident of the rocky escarpments but the ring ouzel (*Turdus torquatus*), once a scarce summer visitor too, may have finally disappeared as a breeding bird in the Burren. Gone too (though not from memory) is the corncrake (*Crex c.*). It was

Cock pheasant – radiant in the morning light.

common in the region until the late 1960s and was recorded from all the 10-kilometre squares during the Atlas survey of 1968-72, but could not be found by 1979. Nowadays occasional calling birds are heard during the summer, but they are so unusual that they draw the attention of the local farming community. Gone too from the region are the partridge (*Perdix p.*) (since the 1970s) and the quail (*Coturnix c.*) (since before 1900), but the introduced pheasant (*Phasianus colchicus*) is common and is constantly re-stocked by gun-clubs into the scrubland.

Birds of prey are still found in the Burren but not, alas, the eagles, which have not been seen in the present century. A pair of (possibly golden) eagles (*Aquila chrysaetos*) occupied the Eagle Rock site on Carran mountain, but nothing can now be traced of their former presence. A pair of white-tailed (sea) eagles (*Haliaeetus albicilla*) definitely bred at the Cliffs of Moher until the 1840s at least. Nowadays the spectacular peregrine (*Falco peregrinus*) occupies these prime nesting locations and there are estimated to be up to six pairs nesting at various places throughout the region. Even these are vulnerable to disturbance, which comes mainly from rock-climbing enthusiasts in the summer. Equally scarce is the merlin (*Falco columbarius*) and its secretive behaviour near the nest-site renders it difficult to locate. The magnificent hen harrier (*Circus cyaneus*) nests in young conifer plantations and is known to have bred in the vicinity of Slieve Elva. Due to the paucity of suitable habitat, it may have vacated the region but individuals are still seen regularly as visitors. The kestrel (*Falco tinnunculus*) and the sparrowhawk (*Accipiter nisus*) are the birds of prey most likely to be encountered in the Burren. The former is the classic hoverer, remaining suspended in the air over potential prey, while the latter ambushes its prey by flying low and fast.

Owls are scarce in the Burren. The barn owl's (*Tyto alba*) favourite habitat is old castles and outbuildings, and as these are coming under increased pressure from developers and renovators the hapless barn owl is being adversely affected. The long-eared owl (*Asio otus*) is found in the scrub where there are trees of reasonable size and in the wooded areas such as Garryland. It goes unnoticed by most people, because its highly nocturnal way of life.

The mature woodland of Garryland has good populations of woodland birds like the redpoll (*Carduelis flammea*), the chiffchaff (*Phylloscopus collybita*) and the spotted flycatcher (*Muscicapa striata*). The Irish jay (*Garrulus glandarius h.*) is also found, but is local. The blackcap (*Sylvia atricapilla*) also breeds there, but it is scarce. It is possible that this woodland may also conceal other rare breeding birds as it is an area that has not been intensively studied.

The birds of the turloughs, lakes and fens

Due to the fact that most of the flowing water is subterranean, Birds like grey wagtails (*Motacilla cinerea*) are rather local. The dipper (*Cinclus c.*) is found in the only substantial surface-running stream, the Caher, which flows out at Fanore.

Turloughs characterise the Burren. They range in size from small ephemeral ponds to extensive temporal bodies of water like that at Carron. The smaller ones are insignificant bird haunts but Carron has numerous wintering and visiting wildfowl and waders. When the water level is low, surface-feeding ducks like wigeon (*Anas penelope*), teal (*Anas crecca*) and mallard (*Anas platyrynchos*) are attracted there. Visiting parties of whooper swans (*Cygnus c.*) and Greenland white-fronted geese (*Anser albifrons flavirostris*) occur also. In times of high flooding diving ducks like tufted duck (*Aythya fuligula*) and pochard (*Aythya ferina*) occur along with coots (*Fulica atra*) and grebes. Wading birds concentrate in the shallows: these are mainly golden plover (*Pluvialis apricaria*), lapwings (*Vanellus v.*) and curlews (*Numenius arquata*) but occasional redshank (*Tringa totanus*) and dunlin (*Calidris alpina*) turn up as well. A few pairs of lapwings and redshanks stay to breed on the dried out turlough in the summer.

The lake system along the eastern Burren, extending from Lake Inchiquin at Corofin to

Skein of Greenland white-fronted geese.

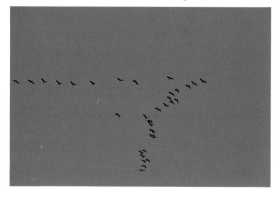

Male grey wagtail in breeding plumage.

Lough Bunny at Boston is an even richer habitat. It holds good winter populations of wildfowl, particularly surface-feeding ducks. Wigeon is the most abundant species with up to 3,000 in Lough Atedaun and 1,500 on the Ballyeighter Loughs. Teal are also abundant but occur generally in hundreds rather than thousands. Mallard is the next commonest, occurring in hundreds. Over 100 shoveler (*Anas clypeata*) have been seen on occasions but small groups are more regular. Gadwall (*Anas strepera*) (up to 20) are found regularly on Lough Bunny. Loughs Inchiquin and Bunny are deeper and are favoured also by diving ducks. Tufted duck, pochard and small numbers of goldeneye (*Bucephala clangula*) occur regularly. Grebes and cormorants (*Phalacrocorax carbo*) may be seen in ones and twos throughout the winter.

Wild swans (*Cygnus* spp.) are found in good numbers in this lake system in most winters. Up to 100 whooper, 100 Bewick's and dozens of mute swans have been seen. Lough Atedaun is their favourite haunt. In October and November 1986, two black swans (*Chenoptis atrata*) were seen there also. Despite investigation, the origin of these swans could not be found. They were full-winged and quite wild and had not, apparently, escaped from an Irish wildfowl collection. It is most likely that they emanated from a British or European wildfowl collection rather than their country of origin, which is Australia. The predominant wading birds throughout the winter are the lapwing which flock to over 1,000 and the golden plover which is found in similar numbers. Curlews are found in hundreds,

Below: top, Lapwing; centre, a lapwing chick camouflaged for survival; bottom, curlew.

Golden plover on spring passage.

Above: snipe in frost. Below: little grebe in breeding plummage.

and while snipe are usually flushed in ones and twos though hundreds undoubtedly over-winter in the marshier areas. In the latter part of the winter or on spring migration small flocks of dunlins, redshank and black-tailed godwits (*Limosa l.*) are seen in the Ballyeighter system. Common sandpipers (*Actitis hypoleucos*) are seen in the spring at Lough Bunny and undoubt-edly nest in the vicinity. Lap-wings, curlews, snipe and a few pairs of redshank breed in the marshy callows and wet pastures alongside the lake system. Sedge warblers (*Acrocephalus schoeno-baenus*) and reed buntings (*Emberiza shoeniclus*) are also common breeders but grass-hopper warblers (*Locusta naevia*) are scarce. Water rails (*Rallus aquaticus*), great crested (*Podiceps cristatus*) and little grebes (*Tachybaptus ruficollis*) breed in suitable habitats.

The extensive fens at Kilmacduagh have been known to harbour breeding pochard (one of Ireland's rarest breeding ducks) and they may hold other secrets besides. It is possible that both the bittern (*Botaurus stellaris*) and the marsh harrier (*Circus aeruginosus*) – now sadly extinct in Ireland – were found there in the past. Both species were widespread in Ireland in the early nineteenth century, but they were perse-cuted and their wetland habitats were drained. Thompson (1850) mentioned that bitterns were frequently on sale at the Ennis market as a food item. Stragglers from Britain are still occasionally shot in winter. The marsh harrier is still occasionally seen but is often shot as well, presenting as it does a strange and soft target to the indiscriminate shooter.

This wetland system is largely undrained and therefore presents the most important wild habitat for birds in the region. Because of the varied degree of flooding which the system experiences, it presents a variety of habitats and therefore of birds, all year round. Over 50 species

are found there in the winter months and similar numbers, but of substantially different species, come to breed there. Disturbance or pollution due to inappropriate siting of housing and their effluent outfalls could alter the attractiveness of this area both for birds and for visiting birdwatchers.

Plumed sentinel – a grey heron in the shallows.

Seabird colonies at the Cliffs of Moher.

The birds of the coast
All year round the Burren coastline is a good place for birds and for birdwatchers to concentrate their attentions.

The Cliffs of Moher, which are not in the Burren proper and are shales and flagstones rather than limestones, are nevertheless so adjacent to our region as to be of interest here. The seabird 'cities' that the cliff ledges play host to in summer have to be seen to be believed and are one of the country's natural wonders. Only on Rathlin Island and in a few other cliff colonies along the coastline can densities of seabirds exceeding those at Moher be found. It is for seabird colonies such as that at Moher that Ireland is of international importance. The most abundant group of seabirds which occupy the cliffs are the auks. Guillemots (*Uria aalge*) are easily the commonest with 4,000 breeding

pairs. About 1,000 pairs of razorbills (*Alca torda*) and a few hundred pairs of puffins (*Fratercula arctica*) also breed there. Of the seagulls, kittiwakes (*Rissa tridactyla*) are the commonest with 1,000 pairs breeding. A few hundred pairs of herring gulls (*Larus argentatus*) also breed there, mainly on the lower cliffs. One petrel species, the fulmar (*Fulmarus glacialis*), breeds abundantly, with over 200 pairs. Shags (*Phalacrocorax aristotelis*), cormorants and black guillemots (*Cepphus grylle*) also nest there but in lesser numbers and so near the bottom of the cliffs that they are often missed. The puffins which nest on the grassy cliff-tops take pride of place with their comical, multicoloured beaks, but they are small and have to be looked for.

But the Cliffs of Moher have other avian specialities too. Choughs (*Pyrrhocorax p.*), those 'personality-plus' crows with red bills and legs nest there (occasionally a pair nest in Gleninagh Castle too). In winter a few can be found at the Fanore dunes. Ireland has a special responsibility for these rare crows, holding as we do the majority of the total western European population. Rock doves (*Columba livia*) are common breeders on the sea cliffs (and on some inland escarpments) in the Burren, and are well represented at Moher. They fall prey to the peregrine which has a traditional site on the cliffs. Ravens also nest there. On the cliff-tops in the less disturbed areas a few pairs of twites (*Carduelis flavirostris*) are to be found. These are rather nondescript little finches. In flight they show a pinkish tinge on the rump; otherwise they look rather like female linnets (*Carduelis cannabina*).

The Moher Cliffs are almost devoid of birds in winter, as most of them are pelagic or sea-going species, only coming to land to nest. Black Head at the north-west extremity of the Burren is a great place for observing seabird movements, particularly after the breeding season. During periods of westerly winds many of these seabirds are forced to fly close by the headland in the course of their cyclic feeding movements, which carry them steadily past Ireland on southerly migration. Many of these birds such as, auks, petrels, shearwaters, gulls and gannets (*Sula bassana*) have bred or been raised in Ireland but many come from farther afield, including the Arctic. Skuas, parasitic seabirds, like sea hawks, pursue and harass the other birds to force them to drop or regurgitate their food. Shearwaters (Procellariidae) from the Mediterranean and the South Atlantic may be seen occasionally accompanying our own species. Little-seen seabirds like storm petrels (*Hydrobates pelagicus*) turn up after gales and may be accompanied by phalaropes (*Phalaropus* spp.), tiny sea-going wading birds from the Arctic which choose normally to swim rather

Choughs foraging on coastal grassland.

than to wade. So when the autumn clouds gather and the winds are high the place to go to see interesting birds is Black Head. Spring is interesting too, but to a lesser degree.

During the winter Black Head is notable for divers, particularly great northern divers (*Gavia immer*). The abundant fish stocks along the north Clare coast can support more than 100 of these massive birds. Loose flocks of a dozen or more are common at Black Head. Red-throated divers (*Gavia stellata*) are less common but do occur in ones or twos. One of the region's really notable birds is the black-throated diver (*Gavia arctica*). Over 40 have been seen together at their regular wintering haunt between Gleninagh and Ballyvaughan. Further east in Galway Bay near the Clare/Galway boundary are found interesting coastal birds like the Slavonian grebe (*Podiceps auritus*) and the long-tailed duck (*Clangula haemalis*), but only a few occur in most winters. These inlets and

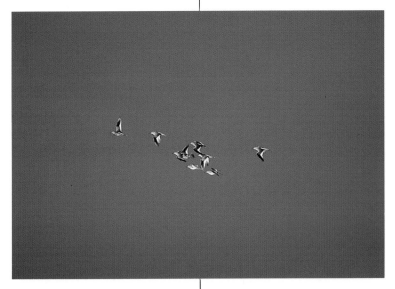

Top: redshank in flight.
Bottom: great northern diver in winter plumage.

muddy shallows also hold wintering Brent geese (*Branta bernicla*), red-breasted mergansers (*Mergus serrator*), shelduck (*Tadorna t.*), wigeon, teal and other wildfowl in small numbers. Wading birds like oyster-catcher (*Haematopus ostralegus*), curlew, lapwing, golden plover, grey plover (*Pluvialia squatarola*), redshank, greenshank (*Tringa nebularia*) and turnstone (*Arenaria interpres*) are also found in small numbers though there is considerable flocking at roosting points.

Birds of prey are attracted to the concentrations of shorebirds. Both the merlin and the peregrine are regularly sighted and the hen harrier turns up occasionally in the marshy areas both along the coast and inland during the winter months.

Stranger on the shore – an avocet. Galway Bay, winter '89/90.

Rare Birds

Rare visitors turn up all over the country and their rate of detection depends to a large extent on the alertness of the birdwatching fraternity. The west of Ireland is generally a good place to look for transatlantic stragglers from North America, and indeed a number of these have been seen in the region mainly after autumnal storms.

Perhaps the most remarkable of these is the belted kingfisher (*Ceryle alcyon*) which occured at Ballyvaughan in the autumn of 1984. It remained for a couple of months and delighted the locals with its strange 'Woody-Woodpecker-like' appearance. At twice the size of our native kingfisher, and with an outsized head and beak, this rarity attracted birdwatchers from all over Ireland and Britain, as it was only the third time that a belted kingfisher had been seen in Ireland. The North American counterpart of our teal, the green-winged teal (*Anas crecca carolinensis*) has been seen at Bell Harbour (1966) and at Killeenaran (1985). Ducks and waders are among the most regularly seen transatlantic stragglers.

The crane (*Grus g.*), not the grey heron which is often called 'a crane' but the much larger bird which breeds in northern Europe and winters in Africa, sometimes turns up in Ireland. One, which stayed a few days in March 1986, found good feeding in the large fields near Newquay on the northern edge of the Burren. It was first spotted by a bus driver and was seen by quite a number of people before it flew off later to a destination unknown. Black Head has produced its share of unusual and rare birds. The pomarine skua (*Skua pomarinus*) and the rare long-tailed skua (*Skua longicaudus*) have been seen, along with the more regularly occurring great (*Skua s.*) and arctic skuas (*Skua parasiticus*). Northern gulls like the glaucous gull (*Larus hyperboreus*) have been seen there as have the little gull (*Larus minutus*) and the rare Sabine's gull (*Larus sabini*). It is likely that Black Head and indeed other areas in or around the Burren will continue to provide sightings of rare or unusual species, particularly with the ever-increasing migrations of birdwatchers.

BOX 10

Birds with distinct Irish sub-species.

The following birds found in the Burren are Irish sub-species and are recognisably different from their counterparts found in Britain:

Irish dipper (*Cinclus cinclus hibernicus*). The Irish race has the rust-coloured band below the white bib but it is less obvious than on the British bird.

Irish coal tit (*Parus ater hibernicus*). Due to the wide range of plumage variation in this species there is debate about the validity of the status of the Irish sub-species. It is generally darker than the British race with a yellowish suffusion on the otherwise white cheeks.

Irish jay (*Garrulus glandarius hibernicus*). The Irish race is noticeably darker and more richly rufous coloured then the British race.

Mammals

The Burren supports a variety of both terrestrial and aquatic mammals which are typical of those found throughout the country. All the land mammals are resident in the region, though half of them are not native, having been introduced into Ireland by man at some stage over the past eight millennia. The marine mammals are all native but in many cases they have a migratory or wandering lifestyle which can cause their sightings to be irregular.

Land mammals

Two land mammals, the pigmy shrew (*Sorex minutus*) and the hedgehog (*Erinaceus europaeus*) are considered to be more primitive members of the class being largely insect-eaters. Both are found in the Burren. The pigmy shrew is fairly common though it is not often seen. It is more often heard squeaking in the grass at the verge of one of the bohereens or from within the grikes. Another favoured habitat is along the high tide line at dusk where they can often be heard foraging for sand hoppers. Hedgehogs favour soil-covered localities with abundant earth-worms, and are consequently local in the Burren. After hibernation, they are encountered mainly in peripheral areas of farmland and farmsteads in the interior.

Ireland has seven species of bats and all have been found in or around north Clare. Recent investigations (over the past decade) has shown some to be surprisingly abundant in the Burren. The Ennis vicinity has revealed good numbers of common species like pipistrelle (*Pipistrellus*) and long-eared bats (*Plecotus*) but also the less well-known Daubenton's (*Myotis daubentoni*) and whiskered (*Myotis mystacinus*) bats. Our largest bat, Leisler's bat (*Nyctalus*

Enveloped by its wings, a lesser horseshoe bat in hibernation.

leisleri), has been found to have significant roost-sites in north Clare. It has long been known that the lesser horseshoe bat (*Rhinolophus hipposideros*) has a distinctly western distribution in Ireland. Overall, it is rare by European standards and north Munster may hold a significant percentage of the entire western European population. Like the other bats, it hibernates during the winter mainly in caves and souterrains (underground chambers in ring forts) which abound in the Burren. It is quite an experience to find these tiny bats in this situation, suspended by their feet from the roof with their wings wrapped around them, Dracula-style. It must be emphasised, though, that they are easily disturbed and should they emerge from their torpid state and fly out into the winter cold, they would probably perish. It is therefore essential that a responsible attitude is taken if the Burren is to remain a stronghold for this, one of its most important denizens.

Both the rabbit (*Oryctolagus cuniculus*) and the Irish hare (*Lepus timidus h.*) are found in the Burren. Despite the dryness of the region, rabbits are not widespread, though they are locally common in the sand dunes at Fanore, at the Rine and in a few other places. The Irish hare, on the other hand is ubiquitous. Hares are found at all elevations from the intertidal zone, where they feed on the succulent, green sea lettuce, to the high plateau where they graze on the rich grasslands. Their early spring sparring bouts are a treat to watch in the open country as they rear briefly on their hind legs, peppering their opposite number with a flurry of jabs (most of which miss the target) and then dash off across the broken ground with astonishing speed and assured footfall. In winter the hares

Irish hares.

lose the 'foxy' red-brown coat of the summer and turn more yellowish-grey. The hind quarters often turn white.

Only four rodents are known from the Burren: the red squirrel (*Sciurus vulgaris*), the brown rat (*Rattus norvegicus*), the house mouse (*Mus musculus*) and the long-tailed field or wood mouse (*Apodemus sylvaticus*). Red squirrels are commoner than might be expected, being found commonly in Garryland, Coole

Red squirrel in conifer.

and in conifer plantations on the periphery of the region. They are also found in the hazel scrub where they fatten up on the natural harvest. Endearing animals to look at, they are detested by foresters for the damage they do to the introduced plantations. They can be encouraged to feed from nut dispensers (for birds like tits) in gardens close to their haunts. Rats and mice are significantly less common in the Burren now than they were in the past, when grain and hay were extensively grown and stored. Brown rats are still to be found near farmsteads, dumps and wherever they can scavenge. Their footprints can readily be found at lakes and along the shore, and some of the islands in Galway Bay, Eddy and Fidgin, are infested with them. The house mouse is also found near human habitation and is only slightly more tolerable than its larger relative. The field mouse is a much more attractive little animal and is widespread in the Burren. Its tawny coat, snow-white belly, large pink ears and feet and shiny black eyes give it a cleaner, more vulnerable image than its 'street-wise' relatives. And vulnerable it is, forming an important diet item for the many carnivores that inhabit the Burren.

Foremost among these is the fox (*Vulpes v.*). Not only is it one of the commonest predators in the Burren but it is also the one most likely to be seen, often during the day. The fox has been a feature in the region for so long that a number of ancient place-names exist, which have been derived from the Irish names **síonnach** and **maðra rua**. But the fox has been heavily persecuted too. Up until 1988, good prices were being paid for

Badger – TB or not TB?

fox pelts and they were hunted at night with powerful lamps and guns. Still classified as vermin by gun clubs, hundreds of foxes are shot and poisoned each year at lambing time. The connection between foxes as predators and lambs as prey is far from established and it is likely that foxes as carrion-eaters do more to help the sheep farmer by clearing up afterbirth and still-born foetuses than to be a pest to him. If the occasional lamb is taken it is much more likely to be sickly or abandoned, for the protective instinct of ewe for lamb is formidable indeed.

The badger (*Meles m.*) is (or was) also widespread and common in the Burren but due to its highly nocturnal habits it is more difficult to find. In recent years, it has been heavily persecuted as a possible vector in the transmission of bovine tuberculosis to the Burren's cattle herds. Intensive study has shown that some badgers do indeed act as reservoirs of the disease but the question of their actually transmitting it back to cattle is far from resolved. The evidence suggests that some hapless badgers are vectors but that open grazing, poorly cleaned-out cattle trucks and other human factors are much more significant. In the meantime, the badger is being killed wholesale despite the fact that it is a protected animal. Its communal lifestyle in the sett labyrinth renders it more vulnerable to eradication than the fox.

Arguably the most beautiful of the Burren's carnivores is the pine marten (*Martes m.*) with its luxuriant brown fur, creamy yellow throat patch and pale tipped parabola-shaped ears. Its cat-like shape and size have given rise to the Irish **caít crann** and place-names like Lios na Gcat testify to its having been a Burren inhabitant for a long time. Indeed, the Burren was until recently its Irish stronghold. It is thought that, with the decimation of demesnes and other woodlands (the natural habitat of the marten), the animal survived by going to ground in remote place like the Burren. Though carnivorous and capable of catching animals as large as squirrels, the pine marten has the most catholic of tastes and has been found to eat nuts, berries and fungi in abundance. Because of its highly nocturnal lifestyle glimpses of this elusive animal are infrequent and many Burren residents have never seen one.

A close relation is the stoat (*Mustela ermina h.*), also common in the Burren. Being diurnal as well as nocturnal it is much more frequently seen. Encounters with a stoat in a stone wall, amongst boulders or in similar circumstances occur regularly, the animal's inquisitive nature often adding to the experience. Like the Irish hare, the Irish stoat is an endemic race, visibly different from its British counterpart. It is warm brown above, white below and with a black tip

to the tail. The brown and white are demarcated irregularly, unlike the neat boundary of the British race, which is also larger. There are no weasels in Ireland, contrary to the public notion. Could the confusion be due to the fact that one of the Irish names for the stoat, *uasal*, sounds like weasel?

An elusive beauty – a pine marten caught in the daylight.

Irish stoat foraging above the shoreline.

Owing to the general lack of surface water in the Burren, otters (*Lutra l.*) are not widely distributed, but they are found in the lake system along the eastern boundary. They are also found along the Burren coast as far as inner Galway Bay. Here they have adopted a marine existence feeding mainly on inshore fish and crustaceans. There are numerous holts along the Burren coastline, notably at

the Rine where otters can sometimes be seen even during the day. Occasional views of otters at play are to be had between Fanore and Black Head, but they are mainly nocturnal and they tend to sleep during the day. The mink (*Mustela vison*), that destructive escapee from fur-farms has spread to most of the country but thankfully appears to have found the Shannon quite a barrier. At any rate it seems not to have reached the Burren.

A dog otter along the coastline.

Though not wild in the true sense of the word, feral goats (*Capra hircus*) certainly adopt wild group characteristics and look the part in the Burren. They are the progeny of introduced animals, which have been allowed to go wild and establish herds. The old males bash heads audibly in the process of establishing seniority and access to the females. Their demeanour is decidedly venerable with their beards and long spirally twisting horns. In the absence of red deer, the native ungulate, the goats act as a natural-looking substitute and contribute aesthetically to the ancient landscape. They serve an important function too in browsing the hazel and other scrub. It is likely that the hazel would have encroached over most of the open limestone (and the flora) long ago were it not for the goats and their appetites.

BOX 11

Mammals with distinct Irish sub-species

The following mammals found in the Burren are Irish sub-species and are recognisably different from their counterparts found in Britain:

Irish hare (*Lepus timidus hibernicus*). The Irish hare is a race of the arctic hare. It differs from its counterpart in northern Britain in being larger and in remaining mainly brownish in winter, unlike the Scottish race, which moults to white.

Irish stoat (*Mustela erminea hibernica*). The Irish stoat is smaller than its British counterpart (intermediate in size between the weasel and the stoat). It is also darker and the white underparts are mottled along the edge, not sharply demarcated as in the British race.

The question of whether or not the Irish otter is a district sub-species of the nominate European otter (*Lutra l.*) has not as yet been resolved. The Irish animal is generally darker and has less white on the face and throat. In the Burren it occurs mainly along the coast.

Marine Mammals

The common (*Phoca vitulina*) and grey seals (*Halichoerus grypus*) are both found along the Burren's coastline. The common (or harbour) seal occupies the inshore parts of Galway Bay and has traditional pupping sites on Tawin Island and Loo Island. Here up to 100 common seals regularly haul out. They also use Deer Island and can be viewed from the Martello tower at Aughinish. Adults adopt characteristic 'banana' profiles as they lift head and tail off the ground when relaxing. Pups are born in early summer and can be observed with the adults on and around these rocky inlets.

Grey seals are visitors to the Burren coastline: their pupping colonies are on the Connemara coastline. Pups are born in the autumn covered in thick white fur, in contrast to the common seal pups which are dappled grey, much like the adults.

Cetacea, the collective term for whales, dolphins and porpoises are the true marine mammals, being strictly pelagic.

Banana bunch – common seals relaxing.

Grey seal.

The commonest along the Burren coast is the porpoise (*Phocoena p.*). Despite being less than 2 metres in length, the porpoise is really a small whale. Small pods of up to a dozen are regularly seen off Black Head all year round. On still days, their exhalation is audible for quite a distance. Dolphins (Delphinidae) are also regularly viewed off Black Head, particularly in late summer and autumn when they appear (like the migrating seabirds) to be following the wandering fish shoals. Though in most species not much longer than the porpoise they an be distinguished by their more dynamic swimming which, unlike the

A dolphin-canoeist encounter off Fanore beach.

porpoise, can take them clear of the surface on occasions. Another differentiating feature is the dorsal (back) fin which in the porpoise is triangular and in the dolphin is swept back in a curve. Usually this can be spotted through binoculars, whereas the differing colours and patterns cannot. The large, greyish bottle-nosed dolphin (*Tursiops truncatus*) is perhaps the easiest to identify and has been spotted regularly off the Burren coast.

It has long been known that whales migrate along the west coast of Ireland, though not generally within sight of land. Due to the success of the whaling industry, this phenomenon is now much reduced. Nevertheless, whales are occasionally stranded on the west coast, indicating that they still migrate as before. Of the commoner species, bottle-nosed whales (Ziphidae), pilot whales (Globicephala) and other small species have been found stranded from time to time on the north Clare coastline. Rarities include the Cuvier's whale (*Ziphius cavirostris*) and the pigmy sperm whale (*Kogia breviceps*), which was stranded in the beach near Lahinch in 1966. A 20-metre (65-foot) fin whale (*Balaenoptera physalus*) was washed up dead on the shore near Black Head in early August 1989. The killer whale (*Orcinus*) is one of the most recognisable marine mammals. The 2-metre (6.5 foot) high, pointed dorsal fin of the males and their black and white pattern renders them unmistakable in the open sea. They are seen from time to time off the Burren coast and are most likely to turn up during the summer months. A male and four females were seen off Liscannor on 1 April 1979; a male and three females off Finavarra on 5 May 1982; and a pair off Black Head in May 1988 for a few days.

Many cetaceans can be identified, using binoculars by features such as size, pattern, colour, fin shape and so on. For those nature-watching in the Burren, they add another dimension to the activity and some time spent looking out to sea from Black Head can prove productive and rewarding.

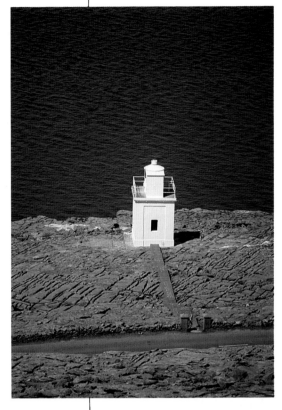

Automatic light station at Black Head.

The Seasons

In the Burren

Not everyone who visits the Burren can do so in spring and summer when the wild flowers are at their best. Those coming in August, for instance, cannot expect to see spring gentians. The Burren compensates, however, by offering the autumn gentian, a less attractive but nevertheless interesting plant. The best time to see numbers and variety of birds, on the other hand, is autumn and winter. Locally reared species, along with passage migrants and incoming winter visitors, are on the move in and around the Burren over this period.

Location is important as well. Both Deer Island and Illaunloo, off the Burren's north coast, are important wildlife haunts, but only for a period in early summer when the cormorant colony is on Deer Island and the common seal pupping is taking place on Illaun Loo. In fact, visitors are not recommended to set foot on these islands at this time because of potential disturbance, but rather to observe from a discreet distance.

Timing and location are important considerations too, in other outdoor activities. Rock-climbing, for instance, when practised on the challenging coastal escarpments in autumn and winter causes little disruption to the wildlife but if practised on inland cliffs in spring and summer it represents a serious threat to some of the region's rarest breeding birds like the peregrine.

This chapter is not intended, however, as a restrictive warning. It is rather a celebration of the Burren's rich wildlife, season by season-a guide to focus the visitor's attention on what is different and where best to go to look.

Left: Dog violets on the woodland floor in spring.
Top right: Blossom before leaf – flowering blackthorn.
Right: Lady's smock, foodplant of the orange tip butterfly.

March–April

The insistent Atlantic airflow across the Burren ensures that the ambient air temperature rarely drops below 4°C throughout the winter months. Consequently, grass has continued to grow on the terraces and on the upland plateaux enabling the age-old practice of upland winter grazing to continue unabated.

Amid the rough grasses and sedges such commonplace plants as daisies and chickweed will be in flower already but it will be necessary to retire to the shelter of the hazel scrub to witness the true early flowering. Here, lesser celandine, wood anemone and dog violet spangle the mossy floor with colour by early March. Look out for the dark-spurred wood violet which is also in flower early. Later in the month celandine accompanied by primroses and cowslips blossom along the south-facing roadsides where shelter is available.

If the winter has been particularly mild some trees will be displaying catkins from the New Year onwards. Hazel, willow, alder and bog myrtle are early catkin bearers. Hazel and alder will be flowering too, long before new leaves grace their fine branches. One of the most striking Burren scenes later in April is the glorious snow-white blossom of the blackthorn. A walk in mature woodland can be productive too. In a few places on the litter of the previous autumn's leaves, and looking more like a fungus than a higher plant, grow the ghostly spikes of bird's nest orchid.

The ponds and freshwater wetlands have their own display of early spring flowers. By the end of March the shiny yellow cups of marsh marigold are beginning to expand along the fringes, and the delicate lady's smock dots the wet green pasture with pale lavender. In April the bright green stiff-leaved fans of wild iris protrude from the wet ground a month or more before they decorate the marshes with their yellow flowers.

Grey gelatinous masses of frogspawn have been accumulating for weeks. By observing from a distance, the frogs, in 'piggy-back' pairs, can be watched periodically emerging from the mass of spawn and disappearing with a 'plop' at the slightest hint of danger. Newts, having hibernated for the winter beneath stones on the dry land, are once again returning to the ponds to carry out the aquatic phase of their life cycle: to raise their young. On drier ground the warmth of early spring breathes life into the Burren's lizards, which are also emerging from hibernation in the grikes and crevices in the limestone. As early as mid-April they can be found basking in sunny weather on the open rock.

Many insects are also emerging from hibernation, but none are more obvious than the butterflies. Some peacocks and small tortoiseshells will emerge in March while brimstones, having overwintered in ivy will respond to the heat of the sun in April. Bumble bees first appear in number at this time too, taking advantage of the early flowers. Male emperor moths, the size of large butterflies, are in flight during the day along the edge of the hazel scrub. Their super-sensitive antennae are scenting out the females which stay hidden until nightfall. By the end of April butterfly eggs will be hatching out and early fliers like the orange tip will be fluttering in the damp meadows.

Among the birds the winter visitors are most obvious. Fieldfares and redwings, with flocks of visiting finches, are gathering in pre-migration flocks in the thorny thickets and hedgerows. Flocks of larks and meadow pipits are dispersing so that they can pair up and breed in the open country. On the wetlands, especially near Corofin, golden plover, lapwings and black-tailed godwits (in smaller numbers) are also gathering in preparation for their return journey to the Arctic. Migrant ducks like shoveler and gadwall may be seen in the east Burren lakes at this time but the wild swans and white-fronted geese are already on their way north to their Arctic breeding grounds. By early April the first sand martins, earliest of our summer birds from Africa, will be hawking for insects over this same wetland. Wheatears can be expected to turn up along the Burren coast; their white tails dancing from rock to rock reveal their presence even before they can be recognised as birds. Mid-April usually sees the first swallows the Burren with their exuberant twittering, and by the last week of the month the cuckoo's unmistakable shout will announce this summer visitor's arrival.

Lesser horseshoe bats, which have been hibernating in caves and souterrains, will be making their nocturnal flights again to catch the hatch of early insects. Other mammals abroad at this time include the tiny pigmy shrew which for the entire winter has been going about its frenetic business. It will expire from hypothermia if it does not eat and metabolise constantly. Indeed it can often be

On silent wings – whooper swans taking to the air.

Opposite: Frog spawning pond.

found dead after a late frost. Of all the Burren's mammals, though, this period belongs to the hare. Groups of females and contesting males can be watched in open country, engaged in their entertaining but bizarre nuptial behaviour. The wide flatlands around Finavarra are as good a place as any in the region to look out for this activity. By the end of April most of the group will have dispersed and the sparring will be over for another year.

Badgers will have given birth in the many setts throughout the region but the young will not emerge for a few weeks yet. The vixen is less nocturnal now and her cubs, which will be born soon, will be brought out into the air even during the day, provided the coast is clear. Dog otters, having adopted their solitary lifestyle after the previous year's cubs were born, are more likely to be seen at this time of the year. Females spend most of their time below ground in the holt; they may give birth at any time during the spring or summer. Pine martens are particularly active at dawn and dusk in scrubby or wooded areas. It is sad that every spring a few are killed by cars on the roads of north Clare.

It is a time of distraction for many of the Burren's feathered and furry inhabitants: care should be taken to accommodate them.

May–June

Provided it has been a normal spring the turloughs will be dried out by early May. Like a dirty bath stain the black moss *Cinclidotus* delineates the level of normal winter flooding. Paper algae or algal 'felt' whitening in the sunshine is characteristically draped over the stones in the turlough bed. In those swallow-holes still holding water grows the strange-smelling aquatic plant stonewort. Though the floor of the turlough is dominated by silverweed and grasses occasional faint specks of colour in the form of violets can be seen. By late May the violet zonation – dog violet; heath dog violet; turlough violet; – will be in evidence in many of these shallow depressions.

Coastal flower arrangement 'au naturel'.

The bright grey limestone has also blossomed to colourful life. The first colour since the latter part of April is provided by the many spikes of the early purple orchid, the bright yellow bird's foot trefoil and the inky-blue milkwort. But here and there across the lightly grazed meadows the tiny, intense blue 'propeller-heads' of the spring gentians are emerging too. By early May they are numerous throughout the Burren. They are accompanied by the velvety-looking catsfoot (mountain everlasting) and the rare dense-flowered orchid in places. Great views of this spring flowering are to be had on the southern and eastern slopes of Slieve Rua and Mullaghmore. Mountain avens is also in full flower by mid-May, and though widespread in the region it is seen to its best advantage on Black Head where, accompanied by sea pink (thrift) and bladder campion, it grows right down to near sea level. Look here also for the saxifrages: both the mossy and the Irish saxifrage grow here in luxuriant profusion along with their smaller but equally pleasing relative, spring sandwort. Most of the flowering splendour is to be found at Poulsallagh (south-west Burren) and includes shimmering yellow carpets of that Burren particularity, hoary rock-rose. By the beginning of June that other famous Burren flower, bloody cranesbill, is commonplace at all elevations throughout the region.

In the sand dunes at Fanore a variety of familiar plants occur including the violets, and on the south-facing slopes the delightful sandhill pansy is in flower. In the hollows between the dunes can be seen the creeping red stems of the parasitic plant dodder. Among its hosts are the common dune plants, wild thyme and bird's foot trefoil.

Preoccupation with the flowers often results in other life forms being overlooked. Insects are especially abundant at this time but only the more obvious are noticed. All five white butterflies, including the dainty wood white (which is the last to fly) are on the wing by late May. In the scrub are the brimstone, the speckled wood and in places, the holly blue and the rare pearl-bordered fritillary. The speckled wood butterfly from the spring hatch is more richly coloured than that from the late summer hatch and the remarkable holly blue is hatched from ivy, not holly, in the second batch. No attempt should be made to catch these insects: with time and patience they can all be identified in the field.

In open country the day-flying moths are helping with plant pollination. There are more than a dozen species, the commonest of which are the heaths, the speckled yellow, and the burnet companion. The flamboyant red and black cinnabar may be about during the day despite its mainly nocturnal habits. In this period it will be laying its eggs on ragwort and in a few weeks the striped black and yellow caterpillars will be feeding voraciously.

By the end of May the stock of summer birds is established. Willow warblers and whitethroats revel in the scrub and thorns where they outsing the resident birds like the dunnock, the robin and the wren. Judging from the frequency with which cuckoos are seen as well as heard they are surely commoner in the Burren than elsewhere in the country. Swallows make their nests throughout the region in farm buildings. Many of the peripheral villages like Ballyvaughan and Kinvara have summer colonies of

Top: Hoary rock-rose in profusion at Poulsallagh.

Bottom: The pearl-bordered fritillary, found nowhere else in Ireland.

house martins. Sand martins are scarcer but nest regularly in the dunes at Fanore. Wheatears are particularly common summer visitors to the Burren's rocky hinterland. In places they share this habitat with stonechats. Rarest of the summer visitors (and latest to arrive) is the nightjar which is still found in one or two undisturbed places. Its strange, far-carrying purring song should be listened for on still nights in June. It should not be mistaken for another summer visitor which also often sings at night, the grasshopper warbler. The song of this bird is much thinner, like the uninterrupted ticking of a fishermans reel. It may be heard in young forestry plantations as well as its more conventional habitat in wetlands.

Of the birds of prey the kestrel is commonly seen hovering in open country. It nests in a few old tower houses and castles in the company of jackdaws and starlings. The sparrowhawk is the other relatively common bird of prey. It nests mainly in trees and often in the refurbished nests of other birds like the hooded crow or the woodpigeon. Other rarer birds of prey which nest (or have nested recently) are the peregrine, the merlin and the hen harrier.

On Deer Island the cormorant colony is a riot to the senses. The sights and sounds of these large and ancient-looking birds combined with the pungent smell of guano has to be experienced to be believed. They share the island with a few pairs of breeding gulls and mallard which tend to leave their nests more readily than the cormorants. A few wading birds, notably ringed plovers and oystercatchers, nest in places along the Burren's coastline. Their speckled eggs are particularly well camouflaged against the shingle background on which they are often laid.

Part of the cormorant breeding colony on Deer Island.

On Loo Island (Illaunloo) the common seals (usually between 50 and 100) gather in May to give birth to their pups. The young have a similar dappled pattern to that of the adults, unlike the silky white pups of the grey seal which are born in the autumn on rocky islets off the Atlantic coast.

The scattered herds of feral goats, so much a feature of the Burren landscape, wander nomadically from one area of good grazing to another. There is a characteristic herd protocol with new-born kids being kept protectively towards the inner part with the females. The sagacious-looking old billies with their long shaggy coats and beards flank the herd and will turn their long, back-curved horns threateningly towards approaching strangers. During the rut the males use this formidable headgear to compete with one another for access to the females. The head-bashing is sometimes so agressive that it can be heard a kilometre or more away from the action.

July–August

Now that the days are long and warm this is a good time to go down to the shore to paddle in the shallows and admire the shore life. The succession of brown seaweeds (wracks) and periwinkles can be easily identified where there is a gentle slope in the inter tidal area. At very low tide the tan-coloured straps of kelp protrude above the water and the seabed is a mass of slow-waving weeds of may colours and forms. In places patches of the bright green sea lettuce occur, especially on the upper shore. The Burren's hares know of this nourishing food source and can occasionally be observed nibbling furtively at low water.

Along the rocky coastline anglers cast for a variety of species of inshore fish like pollack and wrasse. Later in the summer migrating species like mackerel are hooked as they follow sprats and sand eels into Galway Bay. As these fishermen stand with the sea ebbing and flowing at their feet they are often unaware of the marine life in the rock pools. Here an amazing variety of life-forms can be observed in their dramatic life or death existences. Mussels, barnacles and limpets hug the rocks while the surge crashes and drags at them. Packs of dog whelks predate the molluscs leaving tell-tale pin holes in the surface of their shells where they have been 'violated' by the whelk's borer. Purple urchins hide in their excavated hollows protected from all predators except man. Opportunistic hermit crabs don the abandoned homes of topshells and other molluscs and move tentatively amongst coralline algae and sea anemones.

On the flaggy shore near Finavarra gently sloping intertidal habitats exist alongside rock-pool habitats, the juxtaposition creating an ecosystem of extraordinary diversity. If visited at low spring tide the wide reef of Carrickadda can be experienced at its best. Multi coloured weeds grow beside encrusting calcareous algae of a variety of delicate pastel shades. Miniature beaches of maerl (calcareous algal fragments resembling coral) have accumulated in the sheltered spots. Occasional shore crabs and sea slugs stand out vividly in the clear water against the creamy background of the maerl. Some sea slugs (also called sea hares) are blackish with an unusual-looking wavy dorsal flap. They can exude a purplish dye if persistently annoyed.

Rock pool erosion beneath the feet of a lone fisherman.

Dog whelks preying on limpets on barnacle-encrusted rock.

Flowering plants of the Burren's coastline

Left: sea lavender.
Below: sea pink/thrift.

Above: sea radish.
Right: sea campion.
Bellow: sea spurge.

Below: Sandhill pansy.

Right: scurvy grass.
Below: yellow horned
poppy.

Above: sea wormwood.
Left: sea spurrey.
Below: sea holly.

Below: sea aster.

123

Above the high water mark but within the splash zone grow a variety of salt-resistant plants which are often in flower at this time of the year. Plants whose names suggest the spray-dashed shingle in which they are found (like spurge and scurvy grass) grow in conditions which are intolerable to other species. In a few localities the beautiful (but declining) yellow horned poppy will be in flower, its glaucous and fleshy leaves adapted to its harsh circumstances. In more protected conditions (at the Rine saltmarsh, for instance) such plants as sea lavender, sea aster and the aromatic sea wormwood are coming into flower towards the end of the period.

On the open limestone the orchids have come into their own by the beginning of July. Only the withered stalks of the early purples remain but everywhere are the flowering pink and white spotted orchids. Fruity red marsh orchids are more localised and are often accompanied by the greenish-white spikes of the lesser butterfly orchid. Now is also the time to look for the unforgettable insect-mimicking fly and bee orchids, which, in the precise location of the flower-heads on the stalks, have the appearance of something manufactured, not grown. Nor should the delicately scented fragrant orchid be ignored by the orchid seeker. Close relatives of the orchids are equally beautiful. The helleborines are also in flower during this period: the marsh helleborine in damp situations, and the broad-leaved and dark red helleborine in dry situations in the limestone (often in the lee of a stone wall).

The roadside displays of lavender-tinted scabious, sky-blue harebells (pixie-caps), deep-purple knapweeds and somewhat lighter marjoram are beautifully complemented by the jiggling heads of ox-eye daisies and yellow hawkweeds.

Butterflies on the wing include: the dainty small blue (less than 2.5 centimetres (1 inch) across its spread wings) ; the grayling which, with its closed underwings perfectly matching the lichen-covered rocks on which it sits is almost impossible to see until it flies; the dark green fritillary which can be seen on its resolute flights even on top of the Burren plateau. In the meadowland the meadow brown, small heath and ringlet flap lazily about their business. Daytime moths like the splendid six-spot and transparent burnets feed greedily on cushions of wild thyme, safe in the knowledge that their toxic body juices (containing a cyanide compound) will protect them from predators that might be attracted by their bright colours.

In the freshwater wetlands dragonflies are on the hunt. The long-bodied hawkers, the aeshna dragonflies are intricately coloured but difficult to approach; the squat darters are usually monocoloured and easier to view on the wing due to their method of hunting. Mating damselflies, trim-bodied relatives of the dragonflies, are on the wing, linked abdomen-tip to head – in insect acrobatics. Sheltered backwaters are alive with the frenetic scurrying of whirligig beetles and water bugs galore which are supported by the tension in the surface meniscus. Beneath, the diving beetles, upside-down water boatmen, and vicious water scorpions are often visible. The numerous holy wells of the Burren are good places to look for these creatures as are the remnant puddles in the turlough swallow-holes. Look also for eels and newts which, having been confined by the retreating water-table, are often trapped in these circumstances.

Most of the birds have young and are preoccupied with feeding them. Some, like the beautiful yellowhammer are in song into the late summer when cuckoos and others of the Burren's songsters have stopped. Plaintive bird sounds emanating from the wooded thickets may be young sparrowhawks or long-eared owls. In the reed beds and the dense aquatic vegetation of the wetlands reed buntings and sedge warblers are raising families and, in the water below, moorhens, water rails and coots are similarly occupied. These wetlands are very extensive and inaccessible and sightings of certain ducks which are scarce in summer in Ireland, like gadwall, shoveler and pochard, may indicate that they are also breeding there.

Common Aeshna dragonfly.

September–October

Berries and nuts festoon the Burren shrubbery in this season of mellow fruitfulness. On the upper ground the montane plants bearberry and crowberry will already have lost their scarlet and black berries to the birds. But in the scrub, the orange and red berries are ripening on whitethorn, whitebeam and rose, while black fruits are appearing on buckthorn, blackthorn and elder. Nearly all will be devoured by birds and home brewers long before Christmas. Human interest centres more on the blackberry crop. Wild raspberry, dewberry and strawberry are not ignored, though more work is required to obtain tin-can quota. But there are certain berries to be avoided, despite the fact that they can be eaten by birds, like the attractive red berries of guelder rose. There are others too, like the composite pink berries of the spindle tree, which the birds usually leave to the last, holly, of course, and the familiar but poisonous roadside plant lords and ladies.

On the ground fungi sprout from the decomposing vegetation. Mushrooms, including ink caps, milk caps and parasols are eagerly collected

Bearberry.

for the pot along with more familiar field and horse mushrooms. Other less familiar fungi are also edible: honey fungus, velvet shank and jew's ear, for instance. But there are those which are very definitely to be avoided. The golden rule in collecting fungi for the table is to take only those which you know you can eat; not all field guides have good enough illustrations to facilitate positive identification.

One of the Burren's prettiest orchids does not appear until this time of year. The autumn lady's tresses orchid is a 10-centimetre (4-inch) high spike of tiny white flowers that looks as though it has been finger-and-thumb twisted from the top. It is found in short-cropped grassland but because of the strange fungus association required for germination it, like the other orchids, may refuse to flower for several years in a row in a locality where it is known to be profuse.

Elsewhere there is a distinctive assembly of autumn flowers. The pale mauve field scabious is now accompanied by the darker, purple-blue devil's bit. Knapweeds and thistles with their purple heads are widespread and abundant. Hawkweeds, hawksbeards and ragworts look like their yellow-headed equivalents and are equally common. Umbellifers, those long-stalked plants with flattened, umbrella-like flower-heads, are more obvious at this time of the year, other ground vegetation having died back. Typical species in a wide range of Burren habitats are the pinkish-white-topped angelica, the duller wild carrot and the rather finer, white-topped pignut. There are more than a dozen such members of the parsley family found in the region, one or two of which, despite their

Red admiral on field scabious.

benign-sounding family name, are poisonous to eat. In the grassy wetlands there are distinctive autumnal plants as well like the feathery-looking mare's tail which remains bright green when other aquatic vegetation is taking on a decidedly ochreous hue. The most attractive white-flowered grass of Parnassus which is widespread early in the period is almost gone by the end.

Invertebrate life is abundant in the rich rendzina soils and in the hollows where humus is accumulating. A bewildering variety of beetles, bugs, mites and other mini-vegetarians are participating in breaking down the decomposing vegetation. They are being eaten in turn by spiders, centipedes and other carniverous beasties. Aphids, soft-bodied bugs (greenfly and blackfly) are to be found increasingly on the undersides of the leaves of hazel and other trees. Their excreted honeydew is an important food source to butterflies when flowering plants are on the wane. Late butterflies including our largest, the silver-washed fritillary, can be seen exploiting this rich source of nutriment. The brown hairstreak is the latest butterfly to emerge: it can be seen flying around blackthorn in September. But in the brief life cycle that is the butterflies' lot, the next year's eggs will be laid and almost all the adults will be dead by mid-October. Migrant butterflies like the red admiral and the painted lady are also on the wing at this time. They may turn up anywhere but are more likely near the coast. Migrant moths like the hummingbird hawkmoth and the silver Y turn up at this time and may be seen during the day, particularly in coastal areas.

Painted lady on knapweed.

This is an outstanding period for sea birds. Many birdwatchers migrate to Loop Head at the south-western extremity of County Clare but Black Head can be just as rewarding and is much more accessible. By ensconcing oneself on the leeward side of the block-shaped light station at the extremity of the headland it is possible to watch in relative comfort as winds force seabirds to fly by within range. The best time to watch is during or immediately after autumnal storms – the more ferocious the better-but even in calm weather there are many more birds to see now than earlier in the year. On a normal day in September or October long straggling lines of kittiwakes and other gulls, terns, gannets, fulmars, auks and manx shearwaters can be watched battling against westerly headwinds as they move steadily past the headland to the south. These seabirds have bred mainly along the British and Irish coastline and are *en route* to southern and tropical regions of the Atlantic where they will spend the winter.

The familiar are often accompanied by the unfamiliar and occasionally by birds which are rare in inshore waters. The migrating flocks are constantly harassed by those parasitic Arctic seabirds the skuas. They are easily recognised, even at long range, by their white wing-flashes on otherwise dark plumage; their decidedly hawk-like appearance and their dogged aerobatics in pursuit of a free meal. Some of the larger shearwaters – birds from the southern oceans or the Mediterranean – turn up regularly amongst the commoner seabirds, but usually only after severe weather. Shearwaters, with their long, scythe-shaped wings can ride out the worst of the weather despite being driven inshore.

Phalaropes and petrels are equally competent, managing to avoid the worst of the weather by sticking close to the water surface in the labyrinth of troughs between the waves. These sparrow-sized seabirds are a treat to watch within binocular view from Black Head as they apparently revel in conditions that would swamp a ship.

'Seawatching' has other attractions too. A variety of marine mammals can be seen from Black Head and other vantage points along the Burren's coast. Common seals and the odd grey seal can be sighted regularly throughout the year. Daylight otter sightings are scarce and stay vividly in the mind. Cetaceans (porpoises, dolphins and whales) are seen mainly in calm conditions when their rolling backs breaking the surface can be spotted a long way off. Porpoises are the commonest but several species of dolphins and even whales occur. Sometimes, with the upwelling and intermixing of seawater which occurs off Black Head, shoals of fish gather to feed on the abundant plankton. This in turn attracts seabirds such as shags, cormorants and gannets in quantity. Cetaceans are next to appear to feed with the seabirds on the fish. On one such occasion in the autumn of 1989, a number of minke whales were observed participating in the mayhem.

November–February

I am considering the winter as a four month unit, not because the Burren is less interesting (though for the flora it certainly is) but rather because there is a greater degree of uniformity than at other times of the year. The ideal way of experiencing the region at this season is on the basis of a weekend, at least, because of the short hours of daylight.

The low winter light accentuates the contours and escarpments in a singular way transforming the limestone with its essentially horizontal character into a rock-scape of deep, dark, hollows and furrows. The short-cropped grassy terraces are devoid of their summer splendour, though at least for the first half of the period remnants of common plants are still recognisable. Winter storms 'burn back' the thorn bushes, the juniper and the yew growing in the more exposed outcrops. Rainfall (which has been increasing steadily into the period) shines on the whale-backs of the glacially smoothed slopes and gushes out from well-defined spring points (as on the north face of Gleninagh mountain).

With the dying back of the ground-storey vascular plants, and the deciduous shrubs shedding their leaves, it becomes much easier to investigate the mosses, liverworts, lichens and ferns. There are many places in which they can be found together but one of the best is the Glen of Clab and Poulavallan, not far from Carron. Mosses and liverworts cover the boulders like slippery cushions. Lichens, notably the withered-looking dog lichens, grow amongst the mosses while on the bark and twigs of the thorn scrub they are manifestly glorious. A mosaic of crustose and foliose lichens pattern the hazel bark off-white, lead-grey and chocolate-brown while greenish-grey fruticose lichens decorate the twigs at eye level.

Ferns that were physically overshadowed or simply overlooked during the summer now come to the fore, their green fronds standing out against the background of dead vegetation. Hollows between rocks proffer 'swords' of hart's tongue fern while polypody, growing as an epiphyte, thrives in the soggy saddles of the larger trees. Rustyback ferns protrude from the chinks in stone walls.

Their name is derived from the scaly undersides of the fronds which turn rust-coloured with age. Look out too for the smaller ferns. The maidenhair spleenwort and the tiny wall rue continue green and fresh-looking long after the bracken of the open hillsides has died back.

The increasing rainfall has ensured that by the start of winter the turloughs are flooded to a shallow depth. At Tulla (north-east of Turloughmore mountain) the turlough floods to a depth of 10 metres (33 feet) or more but this depth is the exception rather than the rule. The Carron turlough (or polje) is the largest ephemeral body of water in the Burren, often covering 150 hectares (370 acres) of the valley floor. A multitude of dead invertebrates and plant seeds lie on the surface and accumulate at the fringes to form seasonal nourishment on which the wintering wading birds and wildfowl can feed.

Commonest among the waders are the lapwings, golden plovers and curlews though they are often accompanied by a few dunlins, redshanks and a wisp or two of snipe. Thousands of lapwings and golden plovers flock to the flooded pastureland adjacent to Ballyeighter and Atedaun. In this wetland system is found the greatest concentration of wildfowl with hundreds of teal, wigeon, mallard and coots and smaller members of diving ducks like tufted duck and pochard. While the wigeon and the teal tend to concentrate along the watery edges the diving ducks, undaunted by the vagaries of the winter weather, are often to be found in the deepest water. Wild swans and Greenland white-fronted geese eke out the winter in these wetlands: small groups regularly visit Carron turlough. Lough Bunny is deeper than the other wetlands and regularly attracts interesting diving ducks like mergansers and goldeneye. Solitary hen harriers regularly visit the reed beds to hunt for water rails.

Flight of wigeon against a wintry sky.

A visit to the Rine point and saltmarsh can be most productive at this time of year. Many of the birds already mentioned are

Above: Brent geese in saltmarsh. Below: bar-tailed godwit (winter plumage).

found here in numbers. In addition, coastal wildfowl like shelduck, Brent geese and waders like grey plovers and bar-tailed godwits are found. With such a menu to choose from peregrines are regularly seen hunting during the winter.

On the sea in Galway Bay divers are commonplace. The goose-sized great northern occurs usually in ones and twos but hundreds undoubtedly overwinter in the bay (up to 100 can be counted along the Burren's north shore in winter). The rare black-throated diver can be seen here too, sometimes in dozens. Though usually in winter plumage, a few of both species occur in their magnificent summer finery in late winter or early spring before they head off northwards to breed.

Smaller birds are also abundant in winter. Flocks of fieldfares and redwings exploit the richer pickings of the fields in the broad valleys to the north of the region. Skylarks and meadow pipits are still to be found even in the open limestone. The high Burren plateau is almost devoid of birds apart from visiting groups of finches, crows and the odd party of golden plovers.

Linnets and other finches can be found along the shore. Groups of a dozen or more regularly feed on the seed-heads of the saltmarsh plants (like sea lavender) in the early winter. They are thus vulnerable to merlin attack for, like the peregrine, these birds of prey tend to concentrate their efforts in coastal areas during winter.

Beachcombing can be rewarding at this time of year, especially after westerly storms. Besides the variety of shells and tests of marine creatures that are cast up on the shore (some of which make interesting ornaments) there may be some interesting avian flotsam and jetsam. Normally hardy seabirds like auks succumb on occasions to severe weather but more often to fishing nets or oil spillage. Bird corpses should be checked for leg-rings: information, including the address to which to forward the ring number is inscribed on them. Mammal corpses are scarcer but occasionally a hapless otter or porpoise is washed up on the shore in winter.

The winter is hibernation time for a wide range of creatures which, as a survival strategy, entrust their torpid bodies to the sanctuary provided by some nook or cranny away from the worst of the weather. Many invertebrates overwinter in this state, as do amphibians, reptiles and a few mammals. Bats are classic hibernators. The lesser horseshoe bats of the Burren hibernate in caves and in other underground chambers where humidity and temperature is relatively constant. Animals like red squirrels and do not hibernate but are less active in winter. They accumulate stores of non-perishable foodstuffs like nuts and seeds into which they delve as and when the need arises. The population of wood mice in the Burren must be very high for their caches of hazel nuts, typically gnawed open at one end, are widespread in the scrub. The great tit is a specialist at opening hazel nuts; it regularly wedges the nut in the forked branches and taps persistently with its beak until the shell is opened.

Otter footprints in drying mud.

With so many puddles and a reduction in obtrusive vegetation the winter is a good time to look for animal footprints. Foxes, badgers, pine martens and otters have regular noctural runs along which their footprints may be discernible. Each has a characteristically shaped print which, with a little knowledge of what to look for, can readily be identified. For instance, in good prints, hairs can be seen between the pads of fox prints, but not in dogs, badgers' deep prints show long nail-marks, pine martens have cat-like footprints, but nails show and otters have broad, deep pads and the line of the tail may also mark the mud. The droppings of each of these mammals are equally recognisable. Because of their elusiveness the tracks and trails may be the only way of establishing their presence. With the fox, however, the clearly audible courting cries are a feature of the Burren in winter. The dog has a low chuckling "owp, owp, owp", the vixen a blood-curdling, hoarse scream-surely the source of many a banshee story in the Burren.

The Future

For the Burren's Wildlife

*T*he Burren has been known as a floral haven for a very long time. As far back as the seventeenth century travelling botanists like Richard Heaton and the Welshman Lhwyd noticed the flora and wrote about it. There has been a steady litany of discovery since. It was not until the present century, however, with the concentrated efforts of specialists like entomologists, who discovered a great deal about the region's nocturnal moths, that it became recognised as an important ecological entity in its own right. Since the 1950s concentrated work by other specialists has pieced together a picture of its complex ecology and of the wonderful range of life-forms which occupies its habitats.

It would be natural to assume, in view of the attention that the region has received – particularly from overseas naturalists-that the Burren would have been long established as a centre for education and conservation. In fact a perusal of the literature shows that this is not the case. For instance, the Burren was not deemed worthy of consideration in an article: The position of nature conservation in Ireland (O'Ruadhain, 1956). By the time of The Future of Irish Wildlife was written (O'Gorman and Wymes [Eds], 1973) the position was obviously changing and the Burren received repeated mention. Indeed, the past couple of decades have witnessed a general upsurge in interest in the environment. The establishment of new national parks (Glenveagh, Connemara and Wicklow) and the imminent establishment of another in the Burren, the designation of numerous nature reserves throughout the country (including a number in the Burren) which provide statutory protection for additional areas of high scientific interest are further manifestations of this favourable trend.

Education

Evidence of this change is manifest in the recent well- produced, attractive booklets on the Burren which have emphasised aspects of the region like its flora and archaeology. They are tourist-orientated and tend to favour the showy and the spectacular, but as educational aids they have served the public well for the past couple of decades. Some useful educational material was produced by An Rionn Oideachais (1974) in the form of bilingual documentation and colour transparencies and recently (1987) a colour video, The Burren, a Karst Region. Both are rather specific, concentrating on the geological/geomorphological or socio-historical aspects. Undergraduate students from University College, Dublin produced a comprehensive report and audio-visual exhibition in 1985.

The approach was a broad one with many novel aspects. The coverage of the wildlife was, however, disproportionately small.

The Kilfenora Burren Centre was opened in 1975 and has shouldered responsibility for interpreting the Burren to visitors more or less single-handedly since then. The audio-visual representations have increased the awareness of thousands of visitors from home and abroad. Scale models, moulded from fabric and wax, have provided immediate and uncomplicated interpretation for the uninitiated.

In 1976 the Ailwee Cave was opened to the public and has proved to be a Mecca for tourists. Besides the guided tours of the cave (which include reference to the hibernation pits of Ice-Age bears and present-day hibernating bats) there are excellent facilities, including the sale of books, posters and other items relating to the Burren.

More recently, in 1981, an interpretative facility was opened at the Cliffs of Moher – one of the most visited spots in Ireland. On display in the sensitively designed centre is basic material relating to the wildlife found at the cliffs. Perhaps a scale model of the cliffs showing the geology, its relationship to the Burren limestones, its special flora, the relative locations of the breeding seabirds, the antiquities of the cliff-top region etc. could be devised which would more effectively interpret this important location.

The Burren Symposium began in March 1983 at Ballyvaughan and it has been an annual event since 1985. Due to its growing success it was decided in 1986 to hold it twice yearly, in May and October at Ballinalacken near Fanore. The format has been wide-ranging and though emphasising the wildlife, it has included such diverse subjects as agricultural practice and the social history of north Clare. Field trips are a feature of the event. They may include a visit to a fox earth or badger sett (often at night) or may take the form of a boat trip to look for pupping seals. The emphasis on wide-ranging Symposium topics has resulted in a variable quality of presentation, but there can be no questioning its importance as a focus for Burrenarians.

A day-trip to the Burren has become a regular extracurricular outing for many schools in the north Clare/south Galway catchment area. This usually takes the form of a coach trip which transports the children around the interpretative facilities. Though

Rock climbing and conservation – is there a conflict?

ostensibly a most worthwhile exercise, the value is lessened because the pupils are usually of the wrong age group to gain maximum benefit. Most are teenagers and the outing tends to be more an 'escape' from the classroom than a rewarding educational foray. Children of national school age (about 6-12) are (in my experience) most receptive to the natural world and exhibit an individual empathy not yet diverted by examination pressure or puberty. The secondary school curriculum approaches the natural world through the limitations of the science subjects, so failing to recognise the non-academic aspects to which children are particularly empathetic.

If the Burren is to realise its potential as a spawning ground for the environmental sensitivity of future generations it is important that a coherent educational strategy is devised which best utilises both the natural and the interpretative facilities of the region. Moreover, there is a need to revise current methods to fulfil the environmental education requirements of both teachers and pupils. Summer courses for national school teachers on this subject have begun to help, but there is a long way to go.

Third level education is provided for in the two university field centres at Carron (University College Galway, 1975: presently run by Clare V.E.C.) and at Finavarra (University College Galway, 1972). The former, in the heart of the Burren is ideally situated to investigate the Carron polje and the rich flora and fauna in the vicinity; the latter is beside Lough Murree and adjacent to the Flaggy shore, near New Quay. Both these localities have major wildlife significance. These field centres are well equipped with laboratories and accommodation but could perhaps be more utilised, particularly in the winter months. A recent development in regard to third-level education has been the establishment of an agency to encourage university graduates from overseas to come and study in the Burren. As yet (1991) the scheme is in its embryo stage and is relying heavily on local enterprise. There is obvious scope for growth but an injection of funds and backing from a number of universities would be required to allow the project to develop.

Top: field centre at Carron.
Bottom: V. E. C. Field Centre at Turlough.

During the 1980s, the field centre at Turlough came into its own. This environmentally friendly centre (in terms both of design and function) is under the auspices of the County Clare Vocational Education Committee. The centre is involved in a range of outdoor activities from caving to canoeing. Were it not for the environmental consciousness of the staff some of these activities could potentially conflict with conservation interests in the region. A number of other centres and hostels (mostly private concerns) exist in and around the Burren and have regular classes or courses on various aspects of the region's natural wealth. They emerged in response to demand during the summer months but tend to be little utilised in the winter.

Conservation

While fulfilling an important educational role most of the organisations and activities are commercially motivated at their source. Projects like the Ailwee Cave, the Kilfenora Centre, and the Burren Symposium are to a large extent economic enterprises – not that this is to be denounced: anything but. Were it not for the foresight of a few individuals (both locals and 'blow-ins' to the Burren) it is likely that the situation which prevailed in 1956 would be little changed today and the authorities might have underestimated the region's potential. As it is, the tourist authority Bord Failte (latterly Shannon Free Airport Development Company Organisations) has not only recognised its value for tourism but is also well aware of its long-term potential, having worked in conjunction with many of the enterprises. But unfortunately, therein lies the rub. Conservationists are extremely wary of the tourism-style commercial approach to the environment and recoil from facilities designed to 'trap' 'hold' and 'exploit' the visitor.

The Office of Public Works (OPW) became involved in the Burren about 1980 by acquiring some 400 hectares (1,000 acres) of the Mullaghmore district at the south-east. It is anticipated that a small area (presently owned by the conservation organisation An Taisce) can be combined with that area acquired by the OPW to form the nucleus of the proposed national park. It is recognized by the OPW that such a national park should encompass not only the glacio-karstic features like limestone pavements but also grasslands, woodland, scrub and wetlands such as the turloughs, fens and lakes associated with the region. (Many students of the Burren, for instance, regard the wetland system extending along the south-eastern boundary between Boston and Corofin as hydrologically linked to the Burren and therefore part of the system requiring protection

The impact of modern housing on the Burren.

An aerial view of commercial forestry at Slieve Elva.

within the national park). At present the OPW is focussing on this south-eastern sector where they intend to develop the Burren National Park, with interpretative facilities. The short-term objective (nearing completion) is to acquire about 1000 hectares (2,500 acres) with a long-term objective of 2,700 hectares (6,750 acres). It is not the function of the proposed national park to act as a broad protectorate of the Burren as a whole. Its brief is to protect a representative part, or in this case the south-eastern sector less than 10 per cent of the Burren as a whole. Finances are an undeniable restriction, however, and the sector would doubtless be larger were the monies available to acquire more land. (Though similiar in size to Connemara National Park, the proposed Burren National Park will be only a fraction of the size of both Glenveagh and Killarney National Parks).

Legislation does not exist in this country (as yet) which protects areas not suitable nor available for national park-style acquisition like the Environmentally Sensitive Areas (ESAs) in Britain. Consequently a large part of the region (the majority) has no special protection.

An Foras Forbartha, in their 1972 report on the Burren referred to the ecological value of a number of areas within the region and singled out three large areas-the south-west (Ballyryan district), the north-west (Black Head district), and the Mullaghmore district in the south-east-as being of international importance (and therefore worthy of inclusion in any national park structure). Significantly large areas in themselves, these three districts are widely separated from one another and though almost unpopulated, have lightly populated terrain between, including a number of small villages. While protection is quite rightly being afforded to the internationally important Mullaghmore sector what, is to become of the remainder? Granted, there are a score or so areas of scientific interest as listed by An Foras Forbartha in 1980 and now earmarked for or designated as nature reserves under the 1976 Wildlife Act. These areas remain sacrosanct but there has been considerable agricultural and other development in places in between. It would be a great pity if the Burren was ultimately reduced to a mosaic of 'protectorates' surrounded by varying degrees of random development. The effect would be much more hurtful in the Burren than in wooded terrain where the trees can conceal peripheral development. In the Burren it stands out warts and all. Without some kind of 'blanket' protection the Burren is highly vulnerable – more vulnerable perhaps than any other terrestrial habitat in the country.

The Vulnerability of the Burren

A major threat exists in the peripheral erosion of the very landscape that the national park is being established to protect. Land clearance (encouraged by Department of Agriculture grants) intensive fertilising, and other signs of agricultural intensification are taking their toll on the region. With the upheaval evident in western agriculture as a consequence of the limitations of the Common Agricultural Policy, farmers are faced with stark decisions – intensify or diversify. In north Clare where there is the highest incidence of bovine tuberculosis in the country the writing has been on the wall for some years now. Intensification of sheep-and cattle-farming with a dramatic upsurge in silage production since 1986 warn of ominous changes to the traditional, low intensity farming practised in the Burren since time immemorial.

In order that the Burren continues to be as open and accommodating to the diversity of habitats as it is at present, it is vital that traditional farming practices continue on a widespread basis. If, as some people have suggested, all farming activity in the Burren were gradually phased out, much of it would be overrun by hazel scrub which would eventually obliterate the valuable floral habitats. It would remain mostly wilderness, but with a much reduced habitat diversity. Man and his traditional practices are therefore as much a part of the equilibrium of the region as the natural agencies of control. It is thus incumbent on a management body to maintain the status quo – not to encourage depopulation of the region but rather to incorporate the existing population into it. The most convenient (and the most economical) way of implementing this strategy is to pay the farmers a subsidy on condition that they should not intensify their activities. Given that this approach is now being practised in environmentally sensitive regions elsewhere in Europe and is part of EC policy for the future, it can surely only be a matter of time before such measures are incorporated into land-use policy in Ireland.

Unaesthetic as silage clamps and modern hay barns may be they are nothing compared to the visual assault of incongruous dwelling houses. This is particularly true in the Burren where the flat, treeless landscape and wilderness atmosphere is so easily disrupted by modern housing. Though the effect on the wildlife *per se* may be negligible the experience for those looking for the wildlife is immeasurably diminished.

Unnecessarily large and widespread billboarding continues to offend the eye on the by ways and in the otherwise pretty villages of the Burren. If agreement could be reached with all the vested interest, could advertising not be restricted to a few communal signposts and perhaps a directory made available in the premises themselves? Worse, though, than landscape-obliterating signposting are the many proxy dumps in and around the Burren. It is singularly offensive to be confronted with one of these out-of-the-way dumps in the course of a ramble, particularly if they comprise

Below: the impact of land reclamation on the Burren.
Bottom: virgin land being cleared by a bulldozer.

Areas of Scientific Interest

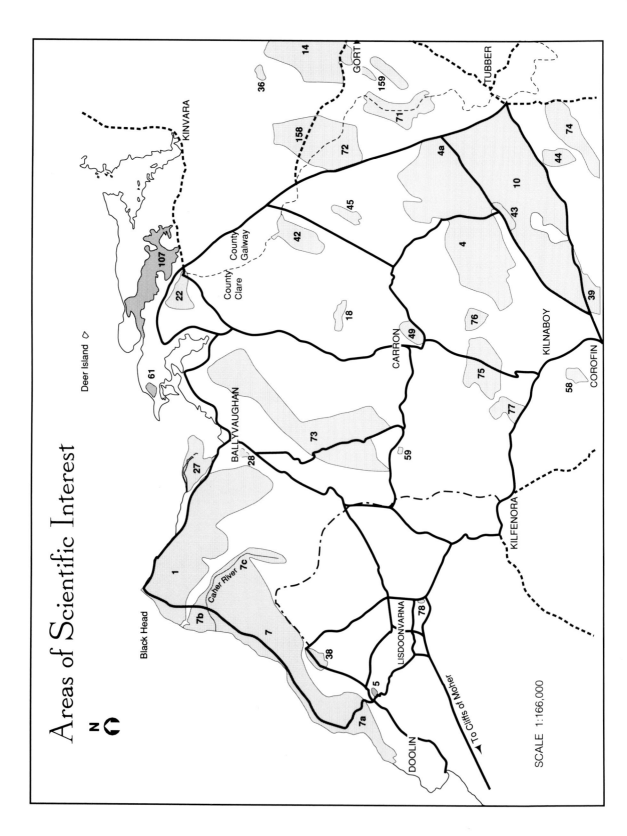

SCALE 1:166,000

BOX 12

The future of the Burren

Areas of Scientific Interest (1987 revision), An Foras Forbartha

1.	Black Head district, Co.Clare
4.	Mullaghmore district, Co.Clare; (4a) Lough Bunny, Co.Clare
5.	Pol-an-Ionain, Co.Clare
7.	West Burren coastline: (7a)Poulsallagh; (7b) Fanore Dunes, Co.Clare (7c) Caher River and valley, Co.Clare
10.	East Burren wetlands, Co.Clare
14.	Garryland wood, Co.Galway
18.	Glen of Clab and Poulavallan, Co.Clare
22.	Abbey Hill, Co.Clare
27.	Rine Saltmarsh, Co.Clare
28.	Ballyvaughan Turlough, Co.Clare
36.	Caherglassaun Turlough, Co.Galway
38.	Knockauns Mountain, Co.Clare
39.	Lough Atedaun, Co.Clare
42.	Slieve Carran, Co.Clare
43.	Ballyeighter wood, Co.Clare
44.	Ballyogan Lake, Co.Clare
45.	Bouleevin, Co.Clare
49.	Carron polje, Co.Clare
58.	Lough Inchiquin, Co.Clare
59.	Kilcorney Caves, Co.Clare
61.	Lough Murree, Co.Clare
71 & 159.	Kilmacduagh Marshes, Co.Clare & Co.Galway
72 & 158.	Gort Lowlands, Co.Clare & Co.Galway
73.	Ballyvaughan Uplands, Co.Clare
74.	Moyree Marshes, Co.Clare
75, 76 & 77.	Clooncoose District and Caherfadda, Co.Clare
78.	Ballyteige, Co.Clare
107.	Aughinish & Corranroe Bay, Co.Clare

Statutory Nature Reserves: (1990)

Ballyteige Hay Meadows (near Lisdoonvarna)	6.4 ha (15.8 acres)
Slieve Carran Uplands and Woods	145.5 ha (359.4 acres)
Garryland Wood	373.5 ha (922.5 acres)
Caherfadda	c 100 ha (c 247 acres)

Besides the above, an area enclosing Lough Murree, Carrickadda, Finavarra point and Illaunloo is also under consideration as a marine nature reserve.

non-biodegradable substances like plastic or glass. The detrimental effect on the wildlife may be insignificant (unless the dumping provides a focus for unwelcome opportunists like rats), but the visual offence cannot be overstated. The well-publicised damage from agricultural refuse can also be significant. Half-buried cattle (victims of disease) can be dug up by carnivores, causing the disease to remain locally active. Run-off from silage pits is intensely polluting and can cause wholesale disruption to wildlife in freshwater wetlands. The wetland system along the Burren's south-eastern boundary is particularly vulnerable and in places where the run-off is underground its damaging effects undoubtedly go unnoticed. Similarly, modern intensification using fertilisers – now evident in the valleys of the Burren – has long-term detrimental effects with a build-up of nitrates and phosphates. Besides, the 'acrylic green' fields treated in this way contrast starkly and in an unnatural manner with the more subtle olive-greens of the wild meadows.

Grant-assisted land reclamation continues annually to reduce the area of open limestone. The efficiency of modern machinery combined with imported topsoil can transform a rock field into pasture in weeks. In recent summers lorry-loads of rock removed in this manner have been transported out of the Burren, apparently for use in rockeries. It is sadly ironic to think of such irreplaceable natural settings being destroyed for the sake of creating floral displays in contrived settings. Land that has been machine-cleared will not grow the characteristic Burren flowers including gentians, orchids, mountain avens, and so on. Instead, invasion by the opportunistic species – daisies, dandelions, and chickweeds occurs. No less insidious is the continuing (though thankfully decelerating) preoccupation with scrub and tree clearance. Copses and hedgerows may be well regarded by some people for their wildlife potential, but to others they are simply an obstruction to agricultural progress. It is often only with the aid of historical documents or by counting tree-stumps, the remnants of cleared woods, that the scale of the loss can be realised. Evidence like hedgerows comprised of elms or understorey trees like holly may be pointers to former deciduous woodlands. Efforts by bodies like Crann are gradually changing public perceptions: people are becoming more aware, more thoughtful of consequences where a decade ago the bulldozer and chainsaw would have been the final arbiters.

The tragedy is that while this thoughtfulness evolves, while the dialogue progresses, so does the destruction by a minority who refuse to become involved despite the sounds of the winds of change. Perhaps pessimism is unfounded. Currently (1991) the EC Habitats Directive is in its final stages of preparation. This piece of legislation facilitates the protection of habitats, flora and fauna by establishing special protection areas (SPAs). An integral part of the directive is the incorporation of traditional land management and the payment of subsidies to farmers involved. Whole regions (like the Burren) would be eligible under this scheme. Let us hope we do not have to wait too long!

Much ado has been made about the Moneypoint Power Station and the threat that it poses to the Burren. While it is important to recognise the fact that acid rain is an automatic by-product of gaseous emissions from the tall chimneys lacking scrubbers, environmentalists have a responsibility to report factually on the likely consequences rather than to use the existence of the plant as a weapon with which to attack development in general. It is much more likely, for instance, that acid rain will affect Dublin or the Midlands of Britain than anywhere west of the Shannon, because of the direction of the prevailing winds (not that acid rain anywhere is to be condoned). Direct local pollution in the form of sulphur dioxide fall out is more likely to reach other localities in County Clare, but the effect on the Burren is unlikely to be significant given the fact that protracted periods of southerly winds are rare. Pollution-sensitive lichens are being monitored at various places in the Burren to see if any change has occurred since operations began at Moneypoint. To date (1991) no change has been recorded that could be attributed to serious aerial pollution. It is possible that more damage was caused by the aerial fertilisation from helicopters which was carried out in the recent past, particularly in the summer of 1983. Nevertheless, the installation of scrubbers into the Moneypoint system would have the positive effect of settling public disquiet in regard to the gaseous emmissions and their potential damage both to human health and to sensitive habitats like the Burren.

The Fate of the Burren

A model for the future of the Burren was produced by the County Clare Regional Development Team in 1986. This report was full of innovation with regard to the sensitive development of the region but in its rather localised approach it was not comprehensive enough to be regarded as a complete development strategy. Among 16 main recommendations was the suggestion that the Clare County Council should become the overall managers of the Burren District. They were to be the formulators of a Special Amenities Area Order and were to carry out environmental monitoring on a range of issues on an on-going basis. However well intentioned these aspirations may be they are far removed from the present-day capability of the county council. Though their ineffectiveness is undoubtedly due more to economic constraints than to a shortage or inadequacy of manpower there is adequate reason to have reservations about entrusting such functions to the council. Take, for example, the removal of dumped vehicles which were to be found in at least 40 different sites throughout the Burren (1989). Though there are legal problems involved in the compulsory removal of such cars and more expense is involved than would seem to be the case, there is really no excuse for the long-term existence of such dumps. On a positive note, the local authorities are, according to Government plans, due for comprehensive review in the early 1990s. It is hoped that outcome of this review will result in the county councils receiving the resources and support to implement

Three examples showing people-pressure at the Fanore dune system, an important floral habitat.

more effectively the considerable powers already vested in them.

The report recommended employing wardens who would act as guides and as guardians of the district. A clever notion too was the proposal to use large boulders marked with an official Burren logo to indicate points of entry into the district – no need for fences! An obvious recommendation was the establishment of a series of walks (based on the existing network of green roads). Information centres were proposed for strategic locations throughout the district with the possibility of an outlier at Kinvara. (At the rate of construction of ribbon development on the west and south-east outskirts of Kinvara this option is rapidly diminishing as a viable proposition). While touching on the agricultural and social aspects the report was sadly lacking in concrete proposals as to how these facets should be moulded into the overall scheme. So too with education. There seemed to be little realisation of the importance of the Burren as an outdoor classroom for both Irish and overseas students.

No mention was made of the need for a Burren conference centre. If the Burren is to achieve the recognition which it warrants, it will need to find a more independent forum than the hotels and public houses which have been its conference centres to date. These establishments have served the Burren well in its 'young' years: were it not for them and the interested people who run them and are part of the region, there would be no Burren Symposium. But the time has come to provide a permanent focus, a nerve centre for the plethora of activities and events which the Burren must surely generate. Of course, this centre would be utterly catholic in catering for all Burren interests. Flora and fauna, geology and geomorphology, archaeology and art, should all be within the ambit of the centre and no Burren-related subject should be excluded from its scope. The obvious location is Ballyvaughan. The ambience of this attractive village, on the edge of Galway Bay and with the entire Burren at its back, is highly suitable for the purpose. Ancillary facilities provided by the town in the form of hotels and other hostelries are also highly suitable. Roads from Ballyvaughan radiate into the Burren's outback making all parts accessible within half an hour by car. It is pointless here to discuss the economic feasibility of such a project. Suffice to say that it is needed and no matter how convoluted the mathematics, the long-term economic benefits in terms of jobs and downstream benefits would far outweigh the initial costs. It goes without saying that the benificiaries should not be merely the inhabitants of Ballyvaughan alone. It would be a fundamental mistake to set up such a project without also developing a mechanism whereby all the Burren's inhabitants should benefit economically. This could be effected by a sharehold scheme open to all the Burren's residents and coordinated by a board drawn from throughout the region.Increasingly, money for projects of this kind is being found from EC environmental funds.

Nor should tourism be undervalued. As our second largest source of revenue (catching up annually on agriculture), it is essential that there is a mature, long-term policy towards tourism in the Burren context. It will not be desirable to flood the region with tourists nor overtly to restrict their numbers, for outside a social framework conservation is relatively meaningless. It is really a question of balance. Consider the Cliffs of Moher, for instance. How many tourists can this beauty spot/wildlife sanctuary sustain before permanent damage is done to it; before the values that are on display for the public are destroyed by those who come to experience them? Already there are signs of cliff-top erosion and other undesirable changes. It is likely in the long run that despite

An overview of the proposed marine nature reserve at the Flaggy Shore, Finavarra.

voluminous evidence from national parks abroad, the Burren will have to learn its own particular lesson. Buffer zones and boundary interpretative and holding facilities are ideal ways of dissipating people-pressure. There are marvellous 'mini-Burrens' in the south Galway region in which a great deal of the wildlife associated with the Burren proper can be found. Coole Park, near Gort, for instance, offers such variety, and extensive deciduous woodland habitat besides. Cuildooish, a 800 hectare (2000-acre) 'mini-Burren' near Ballinderreen (on the main road from Galway to the Burren) offers the same kind of floral and faunal variety.

The Flaggy shore (Carrickadda) near New Quay was recommended as a marine nature reserve in the 1980s. This very special place will add a new, complementary dimension to the Burren. The exceptional variety of marine organisms found there has made its conservation essential. The area of the proposed reserve includes Lough Murree (itself on aquatic environment of special interest) and Illaunloo (the common seal pupping island in Ballyvaughan Bay). Public meetings have been

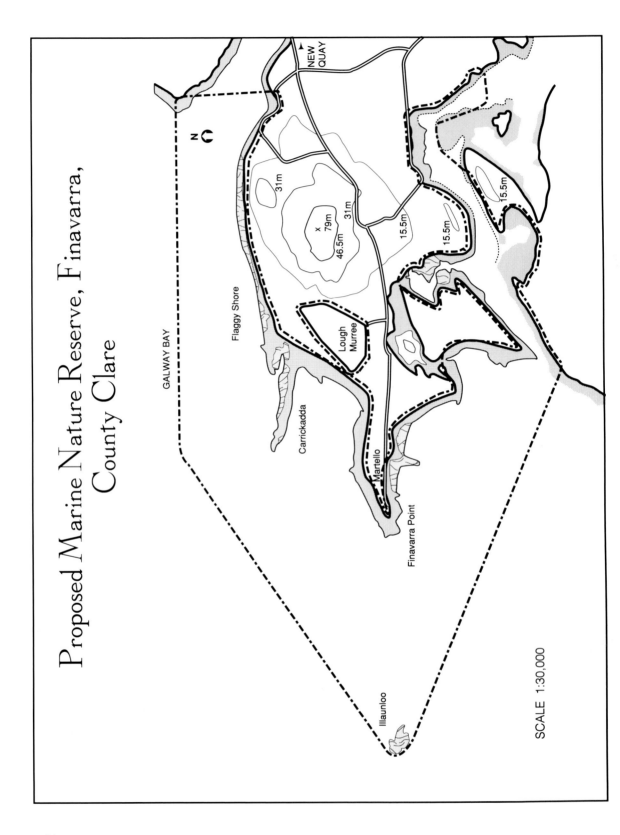

Proposed Marine Nature Reserve, Finavarra,
County Clare

NEW QUAY

GALWAY BAY

Flaggy Shore

Carrickadda

Lough Murree

Martello

Finavarra Point

Illaunloo

31m

31m

79m

46.5m

15.5m

15.5m

15.5m

15.5m

SCALE 1:30,000

held in the neighbourhood to discuss with local people the necessity for the conservation and the possible conflicts over traditional harvesting of shellfish from the shore. The reserve needs to be interpreted for visitors (and locals). An ideal building for this purpose would be the Martello tower on Finavarra point. This fort-relic, designed to repulse an invasion which never occurred would require modification for this purpose but its prominent position would provide a fine overview of the reserve and would facilitate good binocular and telescope views of the seals.

The only other Martello tower, at Aughinish could be similarly utilised providing as it does a fine vantage point from which to observe the large cormorant colony on Deer Island. Acquisition of these privately owned structures has not been discussed but given the co-operation of local people with regard to the Burren in general and the marine reserve specifically the acquisition of these otherwise unused structures is surely within the bounds of possibility.

The 1980s have also seen the emergence of commercial fin-fish-farming. This enterprise which has filled many Norwegian and Scottish inlets with fish cages has met with a mixed reaction in the West of Ireland. In parts of Connemara its establishment has been vehemently opposed, as it has been in Ballyvaughan Bay. It is unlikely, given the level of opposition from crab and lobster fishermen who are concerned about the treatment of caged fish with chemicals that it will gain sufficient local support to become a reality – at least in the near future. Shellfish farming, on the other hand, perceived as being less intrusive both to existing wildlife and also visually: a number of organisations have been involved in shellfish mariculture in Galway Bay since the early 1980s without incident.

The aesthetic appeal of the once traditional farmstead.

The long–term future

Having discussed the immediate conservation potential of the Burren is it reasonable to suggest a possible scenario for the region into the third millennuim AD (or the eleventh millennium PG – post-glacial)? This book has described the wealth of wildlife in the present-day Burren but it has also alluded to the existence of a richer one in the past.

We know from the pollen evidence in the lake beds of the Burren that there were woodland phases during which the thin soils supported birch, pine, hazel and later (mainly in the drift-filled valleys) climax vegetation of oak, elm, ash and yew. We also know from fossil evidence in the caves and along the coast that red deer, wolves, bears and probably wild boar roamed in north Clare in the early post-glacial. Moreover, wolves and deer probably inhabited the Burren into historical times. We also know that white-tailed (and possibly golden) eagles were long-term Burren residents-up until the mid-nineteenth century, in fact. It is possible also that goshawks and capercaillie inhabited the conifer woodlands that mantled the upper Burren into historical times and there may have been others, like woodpeckers, that we now know little about.

Although developing man had more to think about than conservation, this wildlife was nevertheless lost in the name of progress. We must therefore retain responsibility for the resultant impoverishment. The appreciation of past misdemeanours carries with it a moral imperative to avoid further impoverishment.

Assuming that climatic and other fundamental physical, chemical or biological changes do not occur in the near future, it should (with careful management) be possible to maintain the Burren indefinitely as a region of rich, diverse life-forms. Is it sufficient though to conserve the diversity of habitats and species that are presently found in the region, or is there also an onus to re-create? Consider, for instance the fact that the Burren was to varying degrees in the past covered with woodland which was removed primarily by man, what is the desirable degree of afforestation for the region? Should the hazel be permitted to grow vigorously and perhaps develop in places into climax ash or elm woods? What effects would this have overall? Who should make such decisions? It is likely that economic considerations would be the deciding factor in many such matters.

Extensive afforestation on the shale uplands to the south of the Burren is planned by the Department of Forestry (Coillte). At present the blocks of alien species (sikta spruce and lodgepole pine) stand out incongruously against the gentle contours of the limestone plateau. Could this starkly contrasting effect not be minimised by the planting of an outer zone of scots pine, the once native conifer, in a random manner? The resultant effect would not only be easier on the eye but would substantially increase the wildlife potential of these marginal plantations. To some extent this harmonising of the aesthetic with the commercial would be re-creational.

Much has been lost. We can do nothing now about the great auk, extinct as it is to the world, but it may be possible in a place like the Burren to consider the reintroduction of other species eradicated by man. The issue is a complex one and the introduction of non-native species throughout the world have been the source of some of the greatest ecological (and social) disasters. But when it is considered that, for instances, wolves and deer were an integral part of the natural ecosystem in the west of Ireland and would be still were it not for the radical behaviour of man, it is possible to justify their reintroduction. Were this to be done in controlled circumstances, in naturally enclosed areas such as steep-sided hollows, it might be possible (without damaging the values that the region must continue to hold) to display the Burren as it was, for example, when early farmers had to build strong, circular stone habitations to safeguard themselves and their stock from predators.

This is suggested neither as a tourist gimmick nor as a biological experiment but as a valid project, demonstrating the dynamics of conservation. There is a popularly held (but untrue) perception of conservation as an exercise in passive containment. Surely there is more sense to the notion of the reconstruction of what was, rather than the introduction for the sake of effect of what never was – like African safari parks in Cork or Antrim.

Conservation really means keeping options open. In order that the range of options available to a contemporary manage-ment body and to their successors should be wide-ranging the managed area would have to be large. It is therefore of vital importance that the 'wholeness' of the Burren is maintained and that the fragmentation which re-sults in radically differing land usage is curtailed so that this remarkable limestone landscape may be permitted to fascinate, delight and bewilder future generations. And long may the Burren continue to be extensive, its boundaries ill-defined and merg-ing into other landscapes. For once we begin to 'manage' wild places to the extent that they can be readily 'packaged', we are actively destroying that intangible element which makes wilderness so special.

The third millennuim AD is still a decade away. Would it not be fitting if this decade was filled with effort to ensure that, by the beginning of the next thousand years, the integrity of the Burren was sufficiently intact to render its future assured?

Down which road does the Burren's future lie?

Postscript

The Burren belongs to us all. Its protection is far too important an issue to be governed by the perennial problems associated with land ownership. As the globe shrinks and environmental issues such as the expansion of the deserts or the contraction of the rain forests are brought vividly to our attention by the media we are becoming increasingly aware of the value of the earth as our inheritance. As a consequence terms like 'land ownership' are becoming less relevant and are being replaced by 'land stewardship' or 'custodianship' implying transitory, collective responsibility.

The concept of collective responsibility is acutely applicable in the case of the Burren. The local population, the local authorities, state and semi-state bodies and concerned individuals all have a role in the on-going protection of the region. The best mechanism available for this kind of custodianship is the E.S.A. – the 'Environmentally Sensitive Area' designation. The wonderful Mourne district of County Down is covered by an E.S.A. under U.K. legislation but since the necessary legislation does not yet exist in the Republic it is not possible to offer the same protection to sensitive areas here.* The Burren is an ideal candidate for E.S.A. designation and the necessary mechanism must be established without delay to ensure that the values outlined in this book can be allowed to prevail for our benefit and that of future generations.

*Since this report was written, two pilot E.S.A. schemes have been undertaken in the Republic. The larger, which encompasses the Slieve Bloom mountains, is comparable in extent to the Burren and may demonstrate how the latter might be similarly handled.

Bibliography
&
Index

Bibliography

Books

ALLABY M. (1983) *Macmillan Dictionary of the Environment*, Macmillan Press, London

AN ROINN OIDEACHAIS (1971) *Curaclam Na Bunscoile*, ARO, Baile Atha Cliath

BLACK R. M. (1978) *The Elements of Palaeontology*, Cambridge Univ.Press, Cambridge

BURSCHE E. M. (1971) *A Handbook of Waterplants*, Frederick Warne, London

CAMPBELL A. C. (1980) *The Seashore and Shallow Seas of Britain and Europe*, Hamlyn, London

CHINERY M. (1986) *Guide to the Insects of Britain and Western Europe*, Collins, London

CURTIS T. G. F. & McGOUGH H. N. (1988) *The Irish Red Data Book: Vascular Plants (Wildlife Service)*, Stationery Office, Dublin

DE BUITLEAR E. (1984) *Wild Ireland*, Amach Faoin Aer, Dublin

DUTTON H. (1808) *Statistical Survey of County Clare*, Royal Dublin Society, Dublin

ERWIN D. & PICTON B. (1987) *Guide to Inshore Marine Life (Marine Conservation Society)*, Immel, London

FAIRLEY J. S. (1975) *An Irish Beast Book*, Blackstaff Press, Belfast

FITTER A. (1978) *An Atlas of the Wild Flowers of Britain & Northern Europe*, Collins, London

FROST J. (1893) *The History and Topography of the County of Clare*, Sealy, Bryers and Walker, Dublin

GRIFFITH R. (1844) *A Synopsis of the Characters of the Carboniferous Limestone Fossils of Ireland*, Dublin

GUNTHER R. T.(1945) *The Life and Letters of Edward Lhwyd (Early Science in Oxford)*, Oxford University Press, Oxford

HART H. C. (1875) *A List of the Plants Found in the Island of Aran, Galway Bay*, Dublin

HERITY M. & EOGAN G. (1977) *Ireland in Prehistory*, Routledge & Kegan Paul, London

HUTCHINSON C. D.(1989) *Birds in Ireland (Irish Wildbird Conservancy)*, Poyser, Calton, UK

JOYCE P. W. (1901) *The Origin and History of Irish Names of Places (Vols I-III)*, Longmans, Dublin.

MILLS S. (1987) *Nature in its Place*, The Bodley Head, London

MITCHELL F. (1986) *Shell Guide to Reading the Irish Landscape*, Country House, Dublin

McCARTHY P. M. & MITCHELL M. E. (1988) *Lichens of the Burren Hills and the Aran Islands*, Officiana Typographica, Galway

McCRACKEN E. (1971) *The Irish Woods since Tudor Times*, David & Charles, Newton Abbot, UK

NEVILL W. E. (1974) *Geology and Ireland*, Allen Figgis, Dublin

O'CILLIN S. P. (Ed)(1977) *Travellers in County Clare 1459-1843*, Galway

O'CURRY, E. (1861) *Lectures on the Manuscript Materials of Ancient Irish History*, James Duffy, Dublin

O'CURRY E. (1873) *On the Manners and Customs of the Ancient Irish*, 3 vols, Ed. W.K. Sullivan, Williams & Norgate, London

O'DONOVAN J (1838) *Ordnance Survey letters of County Clare*

O'GORMAN F. & WYMES E. (1973) *The Future of Irish Wildlife* – A blueprint for development An Foras Taluntais, Dublin

O'ROURKE F. (1970) *The Fauna of Ireland*, The Mercier Press, Cork

PRAEGER R. L. (1934) *The Botanist in Ireland*, Hodges, Figgis & Co. Dublin

PRAEGER R. L. (1947) *The Way that I Went*, Hodges, Figgis & Co. Dublin

ROSS H. C. G. (1984) *Catalogue of the Land and Freshwater Mollusca of the British Isles in the Ulster Museum*, The Ulster Museum, Belfast

ROYAL DUBLIN SOCIETY (1979) *Atlas of Ireland*, RDS Dublin

SCHARFF R. F. (1899) *The History of the European Fauna*, Walter Scott Ltd, London

SCHAUER T. (1989) *A Field Guide to the Wild Flowers of Britain & Europe*, Collins, London

SHARROCK J. T. R. (Ed.) (1976) *The Atlas of Breeding Birds in Britain and Ireland*, British Trust for Ornithology and Irish Wildbird Conservancy, B.T.O. Tring, UK

SWINNERTON H. H. (1989) *Fossils (New Naturalists Series)*, Collins, London

SYNNOTT D. M. & SCANNELL M. J. P. (1987) *Census Catalogue of the Flora of Ireland*, The Stationery Office, Dublin

THOMPSON W. (1849-51) *The Natural History of Ireland*, Reeve, Benham & Reeve, London

WATTS W. A. (1984) 'The Holocene vegetation of the Burren, Western Ireland', in *Lake Sediments and Environmental History: Studies in Paleolimnology*, Leicester University Press, Leicester, UK

WEBB D. A. (1943) *An Irish Flora*, Dundalgan Press Ltd, Dundalk

WEBB D.A. & SCANNELL M. J. P (1983) *Flora of Connemara and the Burren*, Royal Dublin Society, Dublin, and Cambridge University Press, Cambridge

WOODS C. S. (1974) *Freshwater Life in Ireland*, Irish University Press, Dublin

Journals & Periodicals

Proceedings of the Royal Irish Academy

FARRINGTON A. 'The last glaciation in the Burren, Co Clare', 64(B), 33-9

FOOT F. J. 'On the distribution of plants in the Burren, County Clare', (24), 143-60

GALLAGHER R. N. & FAIRLEY J. S. 'Population study of fieldmice in the Burren', 79(B), 123-37

IVIMEY-COOK R. B. & PROCTOR M. C. F. 'The plant communities of the Burren, County Clare', 64(B), 211-301

JESSEN K. 'The study of the late Quaternary deposits and the flora history of Ireland', 52(B) 85-290

JOHNSON W. S. & HALBERT J. N. 'A list of the beetles of Ireland', 6(4), 535-827

LANSBURY I. 'Notes on the Hemiptera, Coleoptera, Diptera and other invertebrates of the Burren, County Clare, 64(B), 89-115

WEBB D. A. 'Noteworthy plants of the Burren: a *catalogue raisonné* 62(B), 117-34 (Numerous other references by same author)

YOUNG R. '*Tanymastix stagnalis* in County Galway, new to Britain and Ireland', 76(B) Nr 25, 369-78

Irish Naturalists Journal *Numerous references, including:*

CABOT D. 'The green lizard, *Lacerta viridis*, in Ireland', 15,111

MCCARTHY T. K. 'The slow-worm, *Anguis fragilis*, a reptile new to the Irish Fauna', 19(2),49

Irish Naturalist

COLGAN N. 'Notes on the flora of the Aran Islands', (2) 75-8, 106-11

McARDLE. 'Mosses and liverworts', 4 (9), 243-8

Journal of Irish Geography

COXON C. E. 'The spatial distribution of turloughs', 21C, 1, 11-23

HAUGHTON J. P. 'Land use in the Carran polje', 2,225-6

SWEETING M. M. 'The enclosed depression of Carran, Co.Clare', 2, 218-24

WILLIAMS P. W. 'An initial estimate of the speed of limestone solution in County Clare', 4, 432-41

Journal of Botany

NOWERS J. E. & WELLS J. G. 'The plants of the Aran Islands, Galway Bay, 30, 180-3

Journal of Ecology

CLASSEY E. W. & GOATER B. 'Systematic list of the lepidoptera taken in Ireland 5th-9th August 1950'

IVIMEY-COOK R. B. 'The vegetation of the solution cups in the limestone of the Burren', 53, 437-45

MALLOCH A. J. C. 'An annotated bibliography of the Burren', 65, 1093-105.

Journal of Life Sciences

KELLY D. L. & KIRBY E. N. Irish native woodlands over limestone 3, 181-98

WEBB D. A. 'The flora of the Aran Islands, 2, 51-83

O'SULLIVAN A. M. 'Lowland grasslands of Ireland', 3, 131-42

Entomological Gazette *Numerous references including:*

BRADLEY J. D. and PELHAM-CLINTON E. C. 'The lepidoptera of the Burren, County Clare', 18, 115-53

Proceedings of the Belfast Natural History and Philosophical Society

CORRY T. H. 'Notes on a botanical ramble in the county of Clare, Ireland 1879-80', 1880, 167-207

Journal of the Irish Archaeological Society

DINELEY T. 'Dineley's journal from his diary in Ireland (1680)', 6 (1867)

Journal of the Royal Society of Antiquaries of Ireland

WESTROPP T. J. 'Western Europe in the 5th century', 35, 211

Antiquity

O'DRISCEOLL D. A. 'Burnt Mounds: cooking or bathing?' 62, 237, 671-80.

Reports

AN FORAS FORBARTHA Clare County Development Team:
Burren Committee Report, June 1986.
Geography Society of University College Dublin: The Burren, An Exhibition Feb.1985.
School Projects in Coastal Ecology, O'Keffe C. (1971);
Areas of Scientific Interest in Co.Clare (1972);
Distribution Atlas of Ireland's Dragonflies (1978);
Amphibians, Reptiles and Mammals (1979) and Butterflies (1980);
Areas of Scientific Interest, in Ireland (1981) (from National Heritage Inventory of Areas of Scientific Interest, July 1980 and revision
1987);
The State of the Environment Dublin (1985)

BRITISH ARCHAEOLOGICAL REPORTS Int. Series 146, (1982)
DREW D. P. Environmental Archaeology and Karstic Terrains: the example of the Burren, County Clare, Ireland, 115-27 Brit.
Series. 116, (1983)
PLUNKETT-DILLON, E. Karren analysis as an archaelogical technique, 81-94
CRABTREE K. (1982) Evidence for the Burren's Forest Cover (Archaeological Aspects of Woodland Ecology), Symp. of the Ass.
for Env. Arch. 2
IUCN (International Union for the Conservation of Nature) (1978), Categories, Objectives and Criteria for protected areas. Final
Report by Committee on Criteria and Nomenclature, Commission on National Parks and Protected Areas, Annexe to Gen.
Assembly Paper GA/78/24/ IUCN, Morges, Switzerland.
McCARTHY P. M. (1986) Effect of SO2 Pollution from Moneypoint Power Station. Biomonitoring Air Quality in the Burren
University College Galway (1986-)
O'CONNOR R & O'MALLEY E. (1989) Badgers and Bovine Tuberculosis in Ireland (Eradication of Animal Diseases Board), ESRI
REYNOLDS J. D. (1980) Ecology of Turloughs in the Burren, Western Ireland, in Proceedings of the International Wildlife
Congress
SPEIGHT M. (1973) Outdoor Recreation and its Ecological Effects. A Bibliography and a Review, Discussion Papers in
Conservation, 4, University College London)
GILDER P., JACKSON M., WARREN A. (1980) Mullach Mor N.P., the Burren, County Clare. A discussion of the size, location,
management and character of National Parks in the Burren. Discussion papers in Conservation, 27, University College, London.

Theses

BYRNE R. (1982) Ecological Comparisons of Three Water Bodies in the Burren District of Co. Clare, MSc thesis 436, Trinity
College Dublin
CONNOR S. (1989) Impact of Human Activity on the sand dune system at Fanore (Unpubl. Dissertation)
KIRBY E. N. (1981) An Ecological and Phytosociological Study of *Corylus avellana* L. in the Burren PhD. thesis 985, University
College, Galway
MAC GOWRAN B. (1983) The Flora of Turloughs, PhD thesis, Trinity College, Dublin
WILLIAMS P. W. (1964) Aspect of the Limestone Physiognogy of Parts of Counties Clare and Galway, Western Ireland, Ph D thesis
Cambridge University

Index

Figures in **bold** type indicate illustrations.